Your Devil Is Too Big

Your Devil Is Too Big

JEREMY BURGE

RESOURCE *Publications* • Eugene, Oregon

YOUR DEVIL IS TOO BIG

Copyright © 2021 Jeremy Burge. All rights reserved. Except for brief quotations in critical publications or reviews, no part of this book may be reproduced in any manner without prior written permission from the publisher. Write: Permissions, Wipf and Stock Publishers, 199 W. 8th Ave., Suite 3, Eugene, OR 97401.

Resource Publications
An Imprint of Wipf and Stock Publishers
199 W. 8th Ave., Suite 3
Eugene, OR 97401

www.wipfandstock.com

PAPERBACK ISBN: 978-1-6667-1135-6
HARDCOVER ISBN: 978-1-6667-1136-3
EBOOK ISBN: 978-1-6667-1137-0

OCTOBER 14, 2021

THE HOLY BIBLE, NEW INTERNATIONAL VERSION®, NIV® Copyright © 1973, 1978, 1984, 2011 by Biblica, Inc.™ Used by permission. All rights reserved worldwide.

Scripture taken from the New King James Version®. Copyright © 1982 by Thomas Nelson, Inc. Used by permission. All rights reserved.

Scripture quotations taken from the 21st Century King James Version®, copyright © 1994. Used by permission of Deuel Enterprises, Inc., Gary, SD 57237. All rights reserved.

Scripture quotations marked (NLT) are taken from the Holy Bible, New Living Translation, copyright © 1996, 2004, 2007 by Tyndale House Foundation. Used by permission of Tyndale House Publishers, Inc., Carol Stream, IL 60188. All rights reserved.

Scripture quotations taken from the (NASB®) New American Standard Bible®, Copyright © 1960, 1971, 1977, 1995, 2020 by The Lockman Foundation. Used by permission. All rights reserved. www.lockman.org

Scripture quotations marked (ESV) are from The Holy Bible, English Standard Version® (ESV®), copyright © 2001 by Crossway, a publishing ministry of Good News Publishers. Used by permission. All rights reserved."

In honor of my Lord and Savior, Jesus Christ, and my wife, Dana, through which the Holy Spirit used to bring a lost son home. I love you both dearly.

Glory to God in the Highest!

Contents

Acknowledgments | ix
Abbreviations | xiv

1. Why This Topic? | 1
2. You Are Real to Him | 8
3. Fear and Loathing in the Devil | 20
4. Titles Among Men | 31
5. Self-Gratification | 40
6. A World Against | 49
7. Your Future is a Circle | 55
8. L'eggo My Ego! | 65
9. A Final Word | 78

Acknowledgments

NO BOOK WRITTEN IS done so without help from outside sources, influences, memories, knowledge, or experience. Ben Shapiro once quipped that "some books are written over long periods of time, day by day; others are written at white heat." This book falls into the latter category. All my life, I have wanted God to speak to me. Hearing others talk of their experience in receiving a message from the Lord at different times, each in its own unique way, only made me long for it more. Even my wife has her own testimony, to which I will leave for her to tell someday. I remember sitting in my office and feeling a sudden urge, a flooding of thoughts from the Holy Spirit, that turned into this written work. In a period of a little over two months, I had the primary structure for this work and began looking for publishers and working with others to refine the material. I know this now to be my testimony of the Lord "speaking" to me. It was not through any audible sound, but instead it was through an urging of my spirit and fury within my thoughts and fingers. I would like to take the time to say thank you to those that have helped contribute to my journey in life and my development that ultimately led to writing this book.

Thank you to my audience. If you purchased a copy of this book, I want to sincerely thank you for allowing me to occupy your attention and mind for the duration of this read. I hope that, in some way, the Holy Spirit reached you by way of this book. If you

Acknowledgments

have found value in my words and point of view, I encourage you to share this book with others. If for some reason the points of view in this book did not resonate with you, that's okay too. I hope that you continue to search out other books on spirituality and strive to look into other's perspectives and testimonies.

Thank you to the Davenports, for being a blissful memory of my childhood and for welcoming my family into your lives. I remember fondly spending time at your house, playing with your two boxers (which is probably where my desire to own a boxer one day comes from) and admiring the entirety of your Coca-Cola collection, Mister Davenport. Your family made mine feel like we had a sense of community within the walls of Cathedral in the Pines. Your expression of all the fruits of the spirits showed through your work, not only at the church, but with my family as well.

Thank you to Tracee Henneke, one of the very few upperclassmen that I mentioned in the beginning of the book, who actually believed in serving and helping the youth community of Northside Baptist church. I remember her being a strong, positive force for good, living within the spirit and actually trying to help those of us that wanted to understand more about God or helping to mend the division that lived within the youth itself in the form of "cliques".

Thank you to my former mentors, Mayank and Sejal. It was your unabashed faith and testimony that helped lead, not only my wife to the Lord, but allowed the Holy Spirit to work through her to bring me back into the fold as well. Over that 3-year period, not only did we learn specific faith principles, but we also learned business and mindset principles that we will carry with us for the rest of our journey through life. Dana and I will always be grateful for the conversations that we participated in, the wisdom that we were able to syphon, and the reinvigoration of our wills to strive and do more with our lives.

To my editor, Kim McFarden, I am so thankful that God brought you into my life. Not only did your suggestions help with the flow and readability of this book, but your knowledgeable insight within the field of linguistics and structure aided in

Acknowledgments

making this book the very best it could be, and then some. Your dedication and willful determination to help authors realize their vision within the pages of their written work shines brightly. I look forward, God willing, to future collaborations with you.

Thank you to my friends for your encouragement once I revealed that I was releasing a book. Your uplifting comments, rather than those of detraction and disparage, helped to remind me that I had value enough to share with the rest of the world. The conversations that we have had lately and the openness within our relationships has helped immensely to counterbalance a world that does not necessarily want to hear what you have to say if it is not aligned with what they think or believe.

Thank you to my father, Gary, for teaching me so much through the course of my life. I know that during my childhood and adolescent years we didn't not have the best of relationships. However, you and I both witnessed the power of the Holy Spirit as He guided me back to my Christian roots and mended my relationship with you. It's hard for me to know you any differently than my best friend these days. Continuing to learn from you, while also having a chance to speak openly of thoughts and ideas I have and the fruitfulness that is conversation. I appreciate your contribution in helping bring this book to print and your unwavering belief and support of your children, even when our paths looked vastly different from what you would have imagined for us.

Thank you to my mother, Dixie, who was there for me growing up. Willing to have the hard conversations and be a steadfast example of what a strong, spirit filled marriage looks like and how it functions. Your support for me in all endeavors from swimming to playing and singing in the youth group band were always something that reminded me that God had given me great talents. Thank you for waiting patiently as the Lord did his work with me through the years when I was lost and believing that God would keep his promise to help return me one day. I also appreciate your contributions to this book and your input and feedback.

Thank you to my beloved wife, Dana, for taking a chance on me all those years ago, that laid the foundation for our successful

Acknowledgments

relationship and marriage. When I returned to you, in that dive of a bar on S. Manchaca, broken, worn out, doing my best to try and make amends for a life of chaos, I fully expected you to have only met to tell me off, or worse yet, create a scene for your own form of closure. Little did I know, and unbeknownst to you, God had already started His work on you. In those moments when I said sorry for who I was and how I had hurt you, not able to look you in the eyes, I remember vividly you placing your hand on mine and saying, "I forgive you." Surely that was a modicum of what the Lord's grace and forgiveness looks like, and you gave it to me so effortlessly. You have helped our family so much, and if it were not for you and your desire to continue to grow personally, spiritually, and relationally, *we* would not be where we are today. Thank you for being an example everyday of what it looks like to be a strong woman in Christ. For being patient, when your husband is being stubborn or will not listen and allowing God to do His work on me in His time. Thank you for trusting my leadership and helping to show what a great marriage looks like. It is not one that is hoisted upon the principles of singularity, but rather it is a leadership of council. Relying on communication together to ultimately progress forward and achieve the goals we have for our life and family. I appreciate your feedback and notes on this book as well and the belief that God would help this book make its way into the hands of those it is meant. I love you, and I look forward to growing old, laughing, solving issues, raising children, exploring the world and living out loud for Christ, regardless of what the world says.

Finally, thank you to my Lord and Savior Jesus Christ. I knew you for a time and then drifted so far away, and yet you still loved me enough to welcome me back and forget all that was bad and only see the good of what could and will be. I know that I am a sinner and therefore am not worthy of the gift of grace that you have bestowed upon me. Nonetheless, you give freely to those who desire to know you and live according to your word. Thank you for "leaving the 99" to come and find the one lost. I look forward to my continued walk with you through this life, seeing where you lead me and how I can help this world while I am alive. Thank you

ACKNOWLEDGMENTS

for delivering unto me a wife equally yoked within the spirit. A wife that was unafraid to ask me about God and spirituality and to hear my testimony. Thank you for guiding me in that moment to create a space free of judgement and hubris. Lastly, thank you for all my talents, from writing this book, to my abilities in music, whether it's singing, songwriting or playing multiple instruments. For my gift of humor and ability to be a quick study in certain situations and subjects in life. I know that I have achieved nothing on my own, but rather it was from you Father. My greatest desire now is to point back to you and show the world what you have done for me, how you have fixed my life and the redemption and grace I received and continue to receive from you. All praise and glory to you O' Lord always. Amen.

Abbreviations

NIV   New International Version
NASB   New American Standard Bible
NLT   New Living Translation
ESV   English Standard Version
NKJV   New King James Version
KJV   King James Version

1

Why This Topic?

I was raised in the church from the moment I was adopted by my parents until I was eighteen. Like most people I've met who've strayed from the spirit-led life, my *straying* occurred as a teen, when I was still trying to do my best to understand this world. I wanted to know why things worked the way they did. *Why is the sky blue? Why does God do, or allow some of the things He allows?* I was starting to have the kind of questions one might have as their faith world and the secular world began to converge.

I think we can all agree that the teenage years are difficult. Hormones aside, all of these new things awaken within us: new ideas and ways of thinking, an unyielding sense of autonomy and independence, the idea that we can strike out on our own, test the limitations of who we are and see how much we can handle—before we need to return to the solace and guidance our parents provide. This period of time is a crucial point in our lives that, if handled poorly, can cause a chasm between family members, separating those once bound by familial love for years, and in some cases, a lifetime.

So, it became disheartening when some churches I attended operated like a high school social scene, with different individuals and/or groups of people believing themselves to be better than others. My youth group was the epitome of the high school scene: cliques abounded! You had the popular kids who treated others they deemed *lesser* as such. You know, on one side, you had the popular bullies who picked on all the other kids who weren't popular, and on the other side, you had the kids who fell into the category of *lessers* and everything in between: goth, gaming nerds, immigrants, those who appreciated academia and real study of the Bible, ghetto kids, poor kids, kids with mild disorders—nervous tics, hyperactivity, or something within that spectrum—the *just there* kids, and the few sympathetic upperclassmen that actually believed in youth helping youth. It was the same at all the church youth groups I attended, and I attended several.

As I observed, the narrative at most of these churches was, "Don't ask questions, just obey what you hear." This bothered me because, as a teen, I had a lot of questions. I wasn't okay with blind obedience. I desired conversation and interaction with others. I even wanted to find out what others' definitions of faith were, then reflect upon them. Sadly, I never got those answers—or maybe I never asked the right people.

I was starved of these things, and it wouldn't be until I was in my early thirties that I found more people similar to myself—existing in a fog, ambling through life, trying to figure things out. As an adult, I realized that I was allowing societal trends to influence me, social circles to shape my ideological views and ultimately my relationship with God, resulting in my true guidance to wane.

During the time I spent growing up in church, I never had the sense that the congregations my family joined were necessarily keen on new members coming into the community. I think that we can agree, there is a big difference between being *accepted* and being *welcomed*. Aside from the initial greeting we received, which was always very nice, the relationships never flourished. Gatherings outside of church with certain social circles were typically *invite only*. Very few times can I recall my parents being invited to dinners or gatherings. The adults seemed more content with their own separate groups rather than opening up and being inclusive of everyone—just like the youth of the congregation. Could those

Why This Topic?

have also been cliques? Members would gossip about other members, and the congregation dynamic seemed to have this air of little to no transparency about the happenings within the church, such as struggles or congregational behavior that might need to be addressed.

That's not to say that my family and I didn't make friends. In all fairness, there was a relationship or two from which my family benefited and enjoyed fellowship. One such friendship was with the children's ministry pastor and his family, the Davenports. For years, they were a big piece of our lives, and in a way, they became family. Their *good association,* which I will expound on later in this book, still stands as a fond memory for me and my family.

The point of this is, that out of a congregation of two hundred, three hundred, or four hundred plus, having only a handful of relationships seemed to contradict the sentiments of a congregation meant to extend the type of love and fellowship that Christians are called to show toward others. I understand that you are not always going to get along or have friendships with everyone. What I am highlighting is that the *exclusivity factor* that exists in businesses, schools, and society at large, should not exist within a church's community. Do I think that evangelical organizations have addressed this issue and made changes over time, yes! However, do I think that some smaller communities, like where I grew up, could still be suffering from this detrimental way of operating? Sadly, also yes. Even still, my parents were always able to find a foothold within the churches we attended by working as Sunday-school teachers. They also made it a point to be involved in other aspects of the church as well. Whether it was volunteering for fall festivals, camping trips, or youth-oriented outings, they didn't let the dynamics of the congregation get in the way of their desire to help the church.

After graduating high school and leaving home, I did what most frustrated teenagers did, I decided to take a break from church. Why? I was tired. I was frustrated by the lack of answers and meaningful conversations. I was tired of the hypocrisy I saw from people who claimed to follow Jesus but wouldn't have anything to do with you. I was also tired of the whole monotony of it all. Every Sunday morning, every Sunday evening, every Wednesday evening. To be fair, there were fun times and memories made as well, but they weren't enough to counterbalance all that I had grown dismayed with in the church. So, that *break* turned into nearly fifteen years of my life without God at the center. In those fifteen years, I became the very essence of what a worldly lifestyle looked like: I lied, I cheated on girlfriends, I stole, and I spewed anger and hate toward both family and friends. I became a shadow of the person who once prayed to God nightly, sang in the youth praise and worship band, and actively sought to tell others the Good News of the Lord. Inevitably, I let every form of media and technology, as well as secular theologies, lead me through those years.

Toward the end of those dark years, I slowly awoke to who I had become and the things I had done. Who I had become was due greatly to the fact that I had ignored the Holy Spirit's guidance in my life. Instead, I followed what I had learned from social media, film, and other forms of entertainment. I even pursued a marriage with the wrong person. The woman I had chosen to marry did not show any sign of wanting to know God, or desire to examine spirituality as a journey together. As I look back, I can see how this was all part of God's plan to bring this lost son home and back into the fold. He will bring good out of a bad situation if you truly love and have faith in him. "And we know that in all things God works for the good of those who love him, who have been called according to his purpose," (Rom 8:28 NIV).

I once told a good friend, "God works in mysterious ways." To which he responded, "He works in ways that we do not understand, which only seem mysterious to us." In hindsight, when I trace the pieces of the path that led me here, I have come to appreciate the sentiment in this quote. I could never have foreseen the path which I would walk and the actions I would take to *reset* my life, so to speak. Divorce was inevitable, even after extensive attempts at reconciliation, individual therapy, and couples therapy. I understand that God hates divorce; "'For I hate divorce!' says the Lord, the God of Israel. 'To divorce your wife is to overwhelm

Why This Topic?

her with cruelty,' says the Lord of Heaven's Armies. 'So guard your heart; do not be unfaithful to your wife,'" (Mal 2:16 NLT). However, I also know that God wants only good for us, and He does not wish for us to be in a relationship that is inexorably toxic.

On numerous occasions, to my shame, my ex-wife and I not only verbally argued so loud that others near where we lived could hear us, but we also had physical exchanges like throwing things at one another. I wasn't happy and grew increasingly more concerned that I would look up in 5, 10, 15 years and I would be an even more fragmented version of what I had become in that relationship. I felt more than confident that God would forgive me for divorcing and would then move me toward His purpose for my life. "'For I know the plans I have for you,' declares the Lord, "plans to prosper you and not to harm you, plans to give you hope and a future,'" (Jer 29:11 NLT).

After the divorce, I spent time examining the person I had become over the past few years. However, God alone knew that this would not be enough to bring me back to my Christian roots where I could begin to seek Him and rely on His wisdom and strength for the rest of my life. After some time spent developing the new me, I had the opportunity to repair a relationship with a former girlfriend, Dana, who is now my beloved wife. The Holy Spirit used her to bring me back to a relationship with God. I thank God everyday for providing me a wife who desires to learn and grow alongside me.

Divine intervention provided us with a community of people who were unlike anything she or I had ever experienced. People who exemplified Christianity daily, people willing to talk about their faith but never pushing it upon others, and always respecting others' beliefs. Truly, this environment was the complete opposite of what I had known when I was younger. This was where I began a journey to develop a deeper and closer connection to the Lord, while at the same time seeking a way to make a difference in this world.

I began to think about why the world is the way it is. Why do we choose to suffer so much? Why do we continue on a path that continually leads away from God? Why does it seem as if the media is a giant, constantly growing more and more powerful? Whether it's in the form of visual entertainment, be it movies, tv shows, video games, or written and audible entertainment such as books/magazines and music/podcasts. Don't get me wrong, I like movies, sitcoms, game shows, short films, and every other form of media. I just don't let them rule my life or set the bar for my behavior. These have become such powerful forces within our society that people base their morals, ideals, values, actions, and daily lives around what they see and hear in the media as opposed to seeking guidance from God himself.

This brings me to the title of this book: *Your Devil is Too Big!* As I began to write, I recalled a book I had recently read entitled *God's Devil*, by Erwin W. Lutzer. In the first chapter, he posits that we have given too much credit to the Devil in our twenty-first century. I agree! What I mean by *Your Devil is Too Big* is that we have made him intriguing, attractive, complex, interesting, and even empathetic or sympathetic at times. Sometimes, we go so far as to say the Devil can do good and help people! Rest assured, he is anything but *good*. In the very words of Jesus, "The thief's purpose is to steal and kill and destroy. My purpose is to give them a rich and satisfying life," (Jn 10:10 NLT).

Which brings me to the purpose of this book. It has become readily apparent to me in our day and age, that our one true enemy, the Devil, has been given too much credit. Not only that, but our society has let a multitude of things become *new gods* or new devices (both technologically and societally) to keep us *asleep*. Therefore, I want to spend time in this book talking about these *things*. Not in an attempt to tell you what to believe or how to think, but rather to open up a dialogue amongst friends and family. I want to be able to add the value of perspective through what I have come to learn from others who have come before me. This includes books I've read, conversations I've been a part of, things I've listened to, and lastly, time spent with my Heavenly Father, where I believe He imparted wisdom and understanding upon me.

Why This Topic?

My hope is that after reading this book, you will have a different view of some of the things that our world has told us to embrace without questioning. I aim to reset society's perspective of the Devil as portrayed in the various forms of media as well as some of the vital truths our society seems to no longer find important. The world needs to remember, just as I do regularly, who the Devil is, while removing some of the larger-than-life status that is given him, feeding his desires by way of attention and praise. By lessening his status in our culture from a real, menacing, malicious threat, to merely that of a tv character portrayed by the current *flavor of the season* actor, he can begin to subtly convince us that the stories of the Bible are not true, the testimonies are not real, and that God himself is nothing but an empty promise—or worse, that God is not real.

With that said, I have two major hopes for this book. One, that the Lord will guide me through this process. I have never attempted to write something quite of this nature before, and I know that only by His grace will I finish this and have it make sense. Two, that you read this as a companion piece second to Erwin W. Lutzer's *God's Devil*. For it is Lutzer's book that inspired me to undergo the challenge of writing this book.

Lord, I pray you will give me strength, wisdom, knowledge and skill in writing to finish this work for your glory and to help open minds.

Amen.

2

You Are Real to Him

> "I don't believe in the devil."
> "You should. He believes in you."
>
> —*Angel Dodson*
> conversing with *John Constantine*

LIKE I SAID IN the previous chapter, I actually really love movies, tv shows, game shows, short films, and documentaries. When I was a kid, I fell in love with the grand scope of what movies could be and the adventures they could take you on. If you were born in the 80s, then you know what I am talking about. *The Goonies, Batman, Willow, The Neverending Story,* and *Flight of the Navigator* were just some of the movies that, as a kid, I watched over and over. Included in those movies were some of the 80s and 90s most romantic films. Classics, as we know them today. I loved action movies too, but I also loved watching the guy get the girl, the hero save the princess, the mismatched realizing they are perfectly matched.

As long as I can remember, I have had a desire for companionship. To have a wife and, at different points in time, children. I believe this desire came from several different facets of my life. The first being my parents and their strong example of a marriage. Not perfect by any means, *spoiler alert: no marriage is*, but rooted in love for one another and God. Another would have to be coming to know Jesus early in life, though I would ultimately stray for a finite amount of time. I remember in church, youth group, or even at home, hearing the words that God spoke to key figures in the Bible, "Go forth and multiply," inevitably leaving my parents to take a wife and form my own family. Movies also had a huge impact on me as you will see from this chapter, as did seeing people in high school and church dating and having relationships. I wanted to be the hero. I wanted to bring the princess close, kiss her, then protect her and the kingdom for the rest of my days. However, as time went on, that is not what I turned out to be. Really, I became anything but those notions I once held so concretely in my head. At a certain point, because I had kept God out of my life so much, I felt as though none of those things that I once wanted would ever come to be. There was even a brief time in my life where I didn't think I wanted kids.

My parents were a great example of a marriage that worked well. It was *not* perfect; they would argue and disagree over parenting styles, but in the end, they always came back together and included God in their decisions.

Unfortunately, like most teenagers and young adults, I didn't think my parents could teach me anything. Instead, I used romantic movies as my bar for what a relationship should be and a guide for how I should act. I can already hear the boos and hisses. "Rom-coms (romantic comedies) and romantic dramas are great! They end on a positive note!" I assure you, I am a fan of rom-coms and romantic dramas just the same.

The only issue is that, when you decide that the romantic movies you watch will become the lens through which you pursue a relationship or a marriage, you will come to find that they fall short. You see, all movies have the unfortunate task of cramming as much story, hijinks, drama, comedy, character development, romance, et cetera, into a movie that, at most, will run about two hours and forty minutes. However, with the advent of streaming services, movies can be even longer, but that still does not mean they can address or show the resolution of everything, especially when it comes to a romantic relationship or a realistic marriage. The downside of romantic movies, while as great as some of them are, they fail to accurately capture what a real relationship looks like, feels like, acts as. Why? Because in its purest form of art, depicting a scenario or situation, it is still just that, *art*. Said another way, it's a *movie*. Even when the woman is crying, she still looks really good! Why can't I look that good when I cry? It's a movie! The man is shipped off to war, narrowly escapes being killed, and eventually finds his way home to the love of his life. Wow, what are the odds of that happening? Pretty standard actually, when you're talking movie odds.

So, as a kid, I watched those love stories unfold, like *Mannequin*. What an 80s premise if I've ever seen one. Man is a lonely, highly creative artist looking for a job in which he can perform creatively. Woman from the Egyptian time period prays to a *god* begging to be taken away from the prearranged marriage she absolutely does not want. She is placed in present day (80s present day) New York in the body of a mannequin. Only the presence of her true love will bring her to life when no one else is around. Remember the creative guy I mentioned, surprise, that's her true love. Do I like this movie? Of course I do. It's silly and fun. The premise, like I mentioned, is so 80s, and you've got classic, sniveling, young James Spader in it. The only problem is, like most romantic movies, they stop right before the *real* adventure begins. The hero pulls the girl in close and says, "I love you," to which the girl replies, "I love you, too." They kiss, and . . . credits. We never see the work that goes into making the relationship a success, or the highs and lows that the couple inevitably go through. We are just left with the movie assuring us *they make it*. It's no wonder I had many failed attempts at relationships and a marriage when I was using romantic movies as my guide for how things should be.

Some movies, on the other hand, capture the drama—the highs and lows of marriage—very well, but as a kid, you don't quite grasp what is going on. If anything, you're thinking, "This movie is boring." That's not to say that as an adult, I haven't enjoyed more dramatic movies that deal with the complexities of relationships and marriage; however, those should serve as jumping-off points for conversation. We shouldn't be saying, "See that's us!" The characters themselves are similar or akin to us, but they are *not* us. Our situations and circumstances are unique. Not to mention that most secular movies never look at the spiritual end of working on, fixing, and mending relationships, much less a marriage. Most everything is done from a secular view.

Now, you may be sitting, reading this book, and thinking, "Why, in the heck, are you talking about all of this? The chapter is called, "You Are Real to Him," and I am recounting an absurd movie about a girl who's a mannequin, that can be real, but she's not sometimes, and then love and things . . . *why*?

Great question. I want to properly set something up that our world has slowly but surely gotten really good at doing, selling a false bill of goods. It's not just romantic movies in which this happens, it's all media (books, movies, games, audio), and in particular, the media used to depict evil or Satan. In our modern era of *enlightenment*, we have taken it upon ourselves to do one of two things when it comes to depicting the dark lord of despair and lies:

1. We make him incredibly powerful or ugly, or both, to the point where he rivals God himself. He can do many things that refute what God can do, and sometimes, he has that *extra power* to overpower God. He is so menacing and powerful that he can't be stopped. So, we cower in fear biding our time, praying for the Lord to rescue us. On top of all that power, he is incredibly grotesque. Depending on the story being told, with one visual instance being more insistent than the rest, he could have horns protruding from his head and half of a bull's body on the bottom. Maybe he's clacking and stomping around with hooves. Let's throw a bullring in the nose, too. Why not? Don't forget the long black and red cape and trident style pitchfork.

2. He's depicted as sexy. He's the debonair millionaire who's mysterious and elusive. He's *charming*, and when he does

bad things, it's really because he's so *good*, he just had to do something. Inevitably, when his shirt comes off at some point in the film, tv show, or game—because Hollywood—he looks like the guy on the cover of a romance novel about hunky men saving scantily clad damsels in distress.

Are there some truths to these two depictions? Sure there are. Is the Devil grotesque? Yes, but not in his physical appearance. He is grotesque in his actions, mind, and demeanor toward God and mankind. Is the Devil sexy? I wouldn't say sexy, but I would say beautiful, seductive, and suave. The Bible describes Satan as the son of man, the bright morning star, after all, he was one of the most beautiful angels before he challenged God. "Son of man, raise a lamentation over the king of Tyre, and say to him, Thus says the Lord God: 'You were the signet of perfection, full of wisdom and perfect in beauty . . . You were blameless in your ways from the day you were created,'" (Ez 28:12&15 ESV). In this scripture, we are presented with an entity that is the complete opposite of how most, if not all media and artistic representations present the creature known as Lucifer.

This is where the problem lies within our 21st century context. Our media has fictionalized the father of all lies by completely and unabashedly glamorizing him to the point of obscuring our thought processes in regard to who he actually is, and how he can actually affect us. The quote used at the beginning of this chapter is from a comic book movie that I rather enjoyed when I first saw it. Now, some of you that are reading this who know the movie to which I am referring are thinking, "Blasphemy! That movie is inaccurate in every single way!" Frankie says, "Relax!" I agree! That's why when I think of it now, or if it happens to be on and I catch a few scenes from it, I keep in context what it is, a *comic book movie*.

A movie, written by a human being, based on a comic book also written by a human being. That still doesn't mean that there isn't a great line or two of dialogue. The scene in question deals with our protagonist who, at a young age, can see all manner of supernatural things. In his attempt to alleviate himself of this curse, he attempts suicide, only to find out that Hell is real. He is ultimately revived; then, because of the attempted suicide, he spends the rest of his days trying to *buy* his way back into Heaven. He does this by being a warrior on Earth—*exorcising* demons, evil spirits, or anything from the realm of the unholy. As he works to uncover why evil entities are after twin sisters, of which one perishes in the beginning, he begins telling the surviving sister about the war between God and Satan. Her statement back to him is simple but powerful, a reflection of how a good portion of people view the Devil and spiritual warfare. "I don't believe in the Devil," she says. "You should. He believes in you," states our protagonist.

If we take these two lines of dialogue and strip them down, forget the celebrities, forget the movie that they're a part of, and look at the phrases themselves, we can potentially start to see the angle at which Satan himself may be playing to ultimately try and beat God. Spoiler alert! That will never happen! (See Erwin Lutzer's book, *God's Devil*, if you haven't already read it.) What angle is that? Creating a culture and environment built upon and constantly refined with the idea that the Devil is a character. He's not only a character, but a supporting cast member of the world's most elaborately told drama, based on the best piece of fiction ever written which according to some is the Bible. Think about that for a moment. Do you feel that way these days? Doesn't it seem like everywhere you turn, the Devil is just some character that's grossly misrepresented, either in appearance, action, or ability. Wow, we can call those the 3-As! Let's see if I'm right to any degree with this thought. I am going to pause writing for a second and do a quick search online for media involving Satan, and what the premise of these media pieces are about.

Please standby
Elevator Music

I'm back!

First up we have *Good Omens*, a television series based on a novel created in 1990. The premise is that an angel of God and a fallen angel—a demon—have become friends.

Cue audio byte: Aw! Because they have enjoyed life on Earth so much, they are now joining forces to stop the Antichrist and the impending Battle of Armageddon. This is everything to my point. While it's not the Devil himself, it's the supporting players of angels and demons. It's the worldly view that encourages the thought, "Wouldn't it be interesting if angels and demons were actually good ol' buddies? Pals? Amigos? And they're trying to stop the end of the world because, gosh darnit they just love Earthly life so much." Even the name, *Good Omens*, posits contradictory thinking. An omen, by definition, is defined as *an event regarded as a portent of good or evil*. So, the title, if we read it according to the definition, is Good Good or Good Bad. Sorry folks, there's no such thing as good bad. Good is either good, or . . . it isn't. Think about the saying, "so bad, it's good." Is there any way that this statement makes any logical sense? For instance, take cigarettes. So bad, they're good. So bad, that they deteriorate your health, shorten your lifespan, cause birth defects, and change the color of skin, nails, and teeth. But that's what makes them so good? Huh?

Next up *Lucifer*, which began airing in 2016. Can you guess who the story revolves around? In this aptly named TV show, Lucifer has grown bored of his existence beneath the Earth and decides to give it all up. Goin' solo! Gonna head out west and stake his claim as a nightclub owner. But soon problems hit home when he becomes involved in a murder investigation. What's he to do? Well, clearly the most obvious choice—become a consultant to the LAPD. Double bonus, he also winds up appreciating and finding happiness with a female detective on the force. See guys, the Devil's just a regular guy like us. He gets bored and unhappy, and begins looking for the zest of life, as well as someone that he can find and experience happiness with for the rest of his days. Is the picture starting to come into focus?

Last one. The ill-conceived, *God, the Devil and Bob*, which originally aired in 2000 and ran until 2011. God and the Devil are at it again, gamblin' it up. This time it's for the fate of the world. God wants to wipe out all of humanity and start over. However, he realizes that He's just not that type of God. What a revelation! So admirable. Meanwhile, he lets the Devil choose one person with the near impossible task of saving mankind. Enter Bob, a beer drinking, porn watching, auto plant worker, whose only question when presented with this arduous task is, "What's in it for me?" Surprisingly, Bob does the impossible and saves the world. Now, he's God's go-to guy. Numero uno, the big cheese, a consultant ... to God! I think I've given enough examples and context to the idea I stated earlier.

Each of these series and shows has a rabid fan base fully invested in the characters, story lines, production value, and actors involved. What a hat trick, folks! Have you ever met a fan, or even a die-hard fan of a show? They will argue to the death about the show's relevance. They will defend the show's point of view, the characters, and its creators. Sometimes they might even throw out this little gem, "This writer has been such a voice in a time of uncertainty." I've heard this expression before concerning prolific writers and insightful authors and artists. Do you know what a voice in a time of uncertainty is? It's the calm you feel from the Holy Spirit the moment someone bursts into the gas station brandishing a firearm, and you keep calm until the perpetrator leaves. It's allowing cooler heads to prevail—the Holy Spirit to blanket you with control and clarity when your 16-year-old daughter tells you that she's pregnant. *That* is a voice in a time of uncertainty. Let's use an actual recorded example of a voice during a time of uncertainty.

> There the angel of the Lord appeared to him in a blazing fire from the middle of the bush. Moses stared in amazement. Though the bush was engulfed in flames, it did not burn up. 'This is amazing,' Moses said to himself. 'Why isn't that bush burning up? I must go see it.' When the Lord saw Moses coming to take a closer look, God called to him from the middle of the bush, 'Moses! Moses!' 'Here I am!' Moses replied. 'Do not come any closer,' the Lord warned. 'Take off your sandals, for you are on holy ground. I am the God your father—the God of Abraham, the God of Issac, and the God of Jacob.' When Moses heard this, he covered his face because he was afraid to look at God. (Ex 3:2-6 NLT)

So, we have Moses here hangin' out, and all of the sudden, *boom*, a random bush starts burnin'. Like, it's flamin'. It's *mallow flamin'*! Instead of freaking out, like I know I would do because the bush isn't being consumed by the fire, he goes to investigate. Let's really reflect on that for a moment. This random bush that wasn't on fire spontaneously ignites. Then, on top of that, not only does Moses not get weirded out, but he also actively investigates. What are the odds that God was with Moses at that moment? That there was this feeling inside of Moses that said, "You should check that bush out—not run away." It wasn't until Moses heard the voice of God, that he became afraid and covered his face. He did this because he felt that he was not worthy to look upon the face of God. Afraid to look *at*, not afraid *of*. That's a very big difference. Usually it's the other way around. We are afraid *of* but keep looking *at* something. I'm afraid of that scorpion over there but I'm gonna keep looking at it because I know if I take my eyes off of it, it'll wind up on my person somehow—or worse, it will disappear, and then I won't know where it is. But here, Moses wasn't initially afraid of a bush that not only ignited by itself, but didn't burn up, and kept his cool until he heard God's voice. Then, he becomes afraid. For all Moses knew, the bush could have exploded once he got closer to it. But no, he just moseyed on up to it. No big deal. What a great example of a voice in a time of uncertainty.

Now, let's go back to *God, the Devil and Bob* for a moment. One critic said of the show, "*GTDB* offers a more sincere examination of religion than its title implies . . . " Really, a sincere examination? Did anyone happen to catch the glaring contradiction stated within the synopsis of the show? Let's review, shall we? God wants to wipe humanity off the face of the planet but *realizes* that He's not that type of God. Instead, He tells Satan that he can choose one person to attempt to save the world. However, if that person fails, He's going to destroy the world. Uh . . . what? I thought He wasn't *that type* of God—a God that obliterates the world and starts over. Then why is God cutting back-alley deals with the Devil? Deals that still have the outcome of what he wanted to avoid? Such a sincerely confused look at spirituality—truly. What a cleverly disguised attempt at undercutting who God is and the power that he holds. This portrayal paints Him as though He just gained His power last week, that He doesn't actually know what to do or isn't all-knowing, but rather He needs help from human beings. This kind of entertainment has become par-for-the-course and the world is quick to bestow plaudits.

Some eagle-eyed readers will have noticed I stressed the word *realized*. You may even be asking, "Why?" I heard a great quote from Pastor Robert Madu that he may not have meant to be a quote at the time, but when I heard it, I knew instantly how impactful the words he spoke were. He said, "Do you understand that we serve a God that never wonders?" To put that another way, God is never sitting around then all of a sudden saying, "Aw, shucks. You know what I just realized?" If *realizing* were a part of God's character, then he wouldn't be omniscient. He wouldn't be all knowing. To say that "God realized he didn't want to be . . . " implies that God is just as human as we are, and, whoops-a-daisy, He can make mistakes or second guess Himself, too! News flash—not a possibility! "For the word of the Lord holds true, and we can trust everything he does," (Ps 33:4 NLT). Why can we trust everything He does? Because He is omniscient and knows everything. This isn't a build-as-He-goes project. God isn't your dad who says, "Let's take a trip to California; we don't need a map, we'll just figure out how to get there as we go." No, this is the alpha and the omega . . . the original original.

We cannot continue to allow ourselves to become anesthetized by the media, books, or music that paint the enemy of good in light, but rather we should clearly and properly paint him in the shadows where he belongs. Now, again, I can see some of you sitting there, and you're deeply invested in the book and the point of view. Suddenly, though, you think, "Wait, does that mean that I just can't watch movies anymore? Some of my favorite movies are considered classics, and they just don't make them like that anymore. I was gonna show my kids those films!" I'm not saying that at all. Here's what I am proposing: that you *think* when it comes to media entertainment in any form. Can you separate yourself and your ideologies from that of the movies, books, music, and games you enjoy? Meaning, can you watch a movie and remember that it's just that, a movie? Can you ensure that it's not going to embed itself and create a wedge between you and your personal faith, and your belief in God the Father?

I absolutely love the Marvel film series. The way they organize each individual hero's storyline, connecting them to an overall narrative, which culminates in them all working together to stop an invasion on Earth is something of an unprecedented event that shouldn't have worked, but did! If we look closely at two of the main characters, they are portrayed as gods, one a hero and the other a villain. Now, am I to feel bad about watching this film, or that I am somehow disappointing God by enjoying seeing some characters fly around using abilities that God Himself wielded in the Old Testament? I don't think so.

Now, if you start believing in the characters and the stories of Norse and Greek mythology, telling your kids, community, or yourself that they are real, you do yourself and them an injustice. If you believe that those characters do exist and it's just a matter of time before they return and you should start worshipping and preparing now, you are lost. You've allowed the media to blur your understanding of what's real and what's not. If you start reasoning, "Well why would the Norse, Greeks, or even the Egyptians write about these entities or draw pictures of these beings if they weren't real?" If that's where you begin to go in your mind and how you start rationalizing, then, yes, maybe you need to stop watching those types or styles of movies permanently.

I'll be honest, there was a time when I allowed myself to be consumed with the ideas or the narratives that movies pushed out. It got to the point where I almost suspended belief in reality. Ever wonder why there are so many videos on Youtube of kids, and I'm sad to say, adults, who are doing things they saw in a movie that could get them seriously hurt or killed? I'm not judging, I've been there. My comment is not a judgment, it's a question. The answer is because *action star Tom* takes a 30-foot fall but gets up and walks away like he has super immunity when it comes to slamming into concrete. People watch this, and when it comes time to replicate the act they think, "It'll be fine. They do it in the movies all the time!" Have you ever fallen from 30-feet? How about 20-feet? How about 5-feet? I'm not talking about landing on your feet either. I'm talking about just like in the movies—on your side. It hurts! Even at 5-feet, it feels like you were just crushed or hit by a wrecking ball. It doesn't feel pretty. If anything, if you do wind up walking away, you're praying, "Lord, thank you! I will never do that again." We are creating the same effect through ill-fated Youtubers in our next generation. By not being careful about how we present the Devil, or remaining conscious and reminding ourselves about the things we are watching, we miss the opportunity to ask two very important questions:

1. Am I allowing myself to invest too much into the ideological views of the person that created this work of fiction?
2. Am I consciously aware that I am watching a movie, and that, at the end of the day, I hold true to my beliefs and faith in God?

The enemy wants you to forget about him. He wants you to begin to think that he is nothing more than an interesting work of fiction backed by humanistic qualities that beg you to empathize with him and potentially create the emotion of feeling sorry for him.

You may not believe in the Devil.
But the Devil believes in you.
(Paraphrased: *Constantine*, 2005)

3

Fear and Loathing in the Devil

I WAS TALKING WITH my wife the other day, and she mentioned to me that a friend of hers' mom constantly goes to the doctor when she gets sick. What surprises me is that this woman is a devout believer in Christ! What? Really? Then, why always go to the doctor when you get sick? Now, before I get into the topic of this chapter, which explores the power of your words, I'd like to go ahead and state that some of what I'm going to talk about in this section may be hard to wrap your head around. I speak from experience regarding what it's like when we first begin to look at new concepts, ideas, and thought processes, especially when they are within the realm of our own faith and spirituality.

For instance, when I first heard of Joseph Prince and his message on taking Holy Communion, it was hard for me to conceptualize just what he was talking about. After all, all I knew of communion as a kid was that it happened occasionally on Sundays or during major religious service events. More importantly for me, the grape juice they used was so delicious it made me mad that they served it in such little cups! However, Pastor Prince states that we have been using Communion completely wrong this whole time. When we feel sick, we should take Communion and pray to God, claiming the healing that Jesus provided for us by enduring the torture that led to his death on the cross. As a matter of fact, we should pray daily and claim the good health and abundant living provided by God, not just asking him to remove whatever is ailing us or beginning to ail us. Speak it out loud that the ailment is no more! Up until now, I assumed Communion could only be administered at church. Isn't that the way most churches make it seem? "This thing right here? This incredible spiritually-filled act . . . can only be done inside the walls of a church by a pastor or minister." Thank God for Joseph Prince and him being led to bring this truth to light and write a book on it. If you think about it, it makes complete sense.

Was Jesus not sent as a sacrifice for humanity, that we might be able to create a relationship with the Heavenly Father through him? Can you not pray to God any time you want? I just took a second and prayed, thanking God for breathing into me the words and thoughts to use in writing this book. Be assured, I'm not virtue signalling here, I'm lending credence to my point. Do we not have stores that sell unleavened bread like that of which they use during Communion? In case you're in the dark for some reason, the answer to all these questions is, *yes*! So, why in the heck do some pastors give the impression that Communion can only be done within the walls of the church? Because, just like during Biblical times, Pharisees still exist today. What exactly is a Pharisee? Let's look at the definition from *Oxford Languages*:

"*Pharisee*: a member of an ancient Jewish sect, distinguished by strict observance of the traditional and written law, and commonly held to have pretensions to superior sanctity."

Let's see if we can simplify that a bit. A Pharisee is the, "well, actually . . . " guy.

Back in Jesus' time, the Pharisees were the Jewish leaders who people would go to for the settling of disagreements and for clarity on the scriptures and written laws. Just like the definition states, they're the guys at the party that when you're trying to impress a girl you like, and you go barely outside your circle of understanding, they're right there. "Well, actually"—I can't stand that guy.

Your Devil Is Too Big

However, when Jesus showed up, the Pharisees were unable to say, "Well, actually . . . " If anything, they found themselves confused, asking, "What now? What did He say? Was that some sort of riddle with His words?" They did recognize the fact that Jesus was intelligent and knew the scriptures better than they did. They also recognized the fact that the townspeople believed what he said and went to Jesus for answers. It's because of this, that the Pharisees devised a plot to rid themselves of Jesus, so they could go back to the way things were—the days when poor ol' town folk would trip over each other to seek guidance and knowledge from the religious leaders *cuz them just to dumb to gets it*. Of course that's how the Pharisees wanted it, and I think that's how they viewed those they considered *beneath* them. People with power will always struggle vehemently to keep said power, even if they no longer deserve it.

"Wow, the set on this guy," I can hear some of you thinking, maybe even saying out loud. I am not insinuating that *all* pastors, preachers, ministers, priests, clergymen, or clergywomen are like the Pharisees of days past. What I am stating is that unfortunately some people within the religious or spiritual community have allowed the enemy to come in and falsely bolster their egos. Which in turn has slowly begun to derail the congregation that they were charged with guiding. A while back, I heard a great acronym for the word ego: Evil Going On. That seems to fit, does it not? When others have giant egos, what usually happens? They don't listen? Check. They believe they are always right? Check. They stop asking poignant questions of themselves and others? Check. They can't fathom that they wouldn't know how to best handle a situation. In essence, they become a detriment to everyone and everything around them because they listen to no one and do as they please. More on this subject later.

So, just like the topic of communion, some men and women of the religious and spiritual community have presented the Devil as being too big. Reminding us to always be on guard for the one who roams this world and seeks to devour us! Yes, the Devil is out there and he's roaming around, but he's not some towering inferno or giant Pacific Rim-sized Kaju that we cannot take down. "Well, how do you know that this is what's happening, Jeremy? Maybe that's just like, your opinion man." (You're welcome movie buffs.) If this wasn't happening, do you think more spirit-filled and religious individuals, specifically Christians, would know about topics such as the power of your words, sowing and reaping, and the power of Communion in everyday life? I believe the answer to be, yes.

Do you know, it wasn't until I was in my 30s that I read a little book called *Hung by the Tongue* by Francis P. Martin. Not one pastor, decon, youth minister, or congregation member in any of the churches I attended ever seriously examined and preached on any of the three topics mentioned above. And the kicker? Each one of them is in the Bible. Isn't the Bible our manual directly from God, himself? Our *almanac*, so to speak, that's available to us for daily reading and study, or when we are uncertain and find ourselves lost? Sure does seem like there's information and guidance being withheld from those who are supposed to be helping us in creating a community in which we can freely talk and ask questions.

When our present clergy neglect to tell us of things like these, and instead remind us to give to the church, or they play to the middle of the road as not to offend anybody, they inadvertently aid the enemy, which continues to lend to this narrative that he is larger than life. When pastors or preachers hear people in their congregation say things like, "I just don't know about this pandemic. Things are getting really bad." Or, "We are hoping Steven gets into a good college, but he's just never been a good test taker." They should immediately correct the individual and speak life over whatever situation is being discussed, and then teach why our words are important. If you are a pastor or are in charge of a congregation, and by the grace of God Himself are reading this book, please, educate your congregation and staff on the power of words. Have you taken the temp of the world lately? People are just throwing around their words as if they are nothing. My gosh, what a dangerous thought process! And this is where we begin to examine what the power of words and what that looks like in application within our own lives.

Your Devil Is Too Big

I heard a very knowledgeable person on Instagram (don't laugh, there are actually *some* wise individuals) state that when we speak, our words exist forever, out in the world. Let's see if we can prove that, okay? One of my favorite classes in college, and there were not many, was physics. I 100% believe in God. That doesn't mean that I don't enjoy seeing and understanding how things work. God made everything, and He also made everything to work together. Why do you think science is so interesting to some people? Because when you start to see how things work, it's amazing and extremely intricate. Because God's an amazing and intricate God that knows what He's doing. Come on now, ya'll!

Back to the task at hand. We're talking about proving if when you speak and your words leave your mouth, that those words continue to exist in the world forever. When you actuate the muscle to speak, you use energy to flex your vocal cords, or vocal folds. These twin bands of muscle composed of mucous membrane are found within your vocal box, or larynx. The cords vibrate from the energy you used via the thought process, causing air from the lungs to pass through the cords, which make the sounds that come out of your mouth. Our mouth and our tongue help create definition in the sounds, creating words, letters, and phrases.

So, what does science say about energy? *Energy cannot be created or destroyed, only conserved.* The energy your body generated to speak was conservative energy that already existed within, because we are walking energies constantly in motion. Even when we sleep our body is still moving on the inside. Our gastrointestinal tract is digesting the food we ate at dinner or perhaps that late night snack. Our brains are doing a memory dump of the day's events, deciphering what's important and what's not. Our body as a whole, is mending and repairing itself for the forthcoming day. All of this takes energy.

The last pieces of the equation are the words themselves. What are those sounds classified as? Energy. Energy comes in two forms: potential and kinetic. Potential energy is aptly expressed in the name. It is the energy that potentially exists in an object or person if it were to act on another object or person. Think about a 20lb weight suspended in the air by a rope. The potential energy of that weight is not based on its own weight but its position relative to the object in which it will make contact, in this case, the floor. When the rope is cut and the weight smashes into the floor, we observe kinetic energy. That kinetic energy is transferred into another type of energy, in this case, it would most likely be the *thud* made from the collision with the floor. Sound energy is still energy, meaning that it, too, cannot be destroyed. We may not be able to audibly hear it anymore, but the energy itself still exists. With these things in mind, I think it would be safe to concur that the statement, *words last forever* is both sound and true.

Some of you right now are like, "Whoa..." straight up Keanu style. Others are probably saying, "Ya bro, we get it, you know some science." A small select few of you are currently looking for my address online, so you can school me in physics because, in your opinion, I am off-base on some things, and the scientist inside you must correct me. Here, let's try a simpler example then. How many of you have ever heard stories of friends, parents, siblings, ex-husbands, and ex-wives that have gone to their graves holding onto things people said to them, or arguments they had that they just couldn't get over? I would be willing to bet with varying degrees, a good portion of us probably have heard such stories. Even worse is the fact that usually feuds like that don't just stay with one person. It is usually discussed within the family. Don't think so? How many times have you seen hatred carried down from generation to generation? How do you think that hatred got there? People don't just come out of the womb hating other people. It's a learned behavior from their family or environment. Things like this happen when you are forced as a child to be around your family. Believe it or not, a lot of children still reside in homes of abuse, neglect, poor disciplinary methods, or the adults inability to keep the drama of life or the family within the confines of adult conversations. For instance, I never knew the drama that existed in my family until I was older (and it's not like there was some huge amount of it), because my parents talked about such conversations within the privacy of their own bedroom, or when the kids were asleep or away. Another area in which this can take place is school. While school is a great place to make friends, you are also limited by the selection of those from which to choose. Working in the education system for the last 12 years, I can attest that I have seen more than one *good* kid befriend the group of *bad* kids. While the child makes the choice, the allure is always the same: belonging. I will discuss this more later in the book.

"I'm not sure what you're talking about. Is this thing like a pencil or not? Is there a point?" Sorry, I had to throw in some levity for a moment. All jokes aside though, what are the odds that the Devil knows of these things? That he uses them as strategies when it is beneficial for him to do so. Let's take a look at our manual once again. What does our Heavenly Father say about our words? "The tongue can bring death or life; those who love to talk will reap the consequences," (Prv 18:21 NLT). Or how about this one: "A gentle answer turns away wrath, but a harsh word stirs up anger," (Prv 15:1 NAB).

Why are these verses important? It shows that God gave us the ability to speak positive over the negative. Everything that is negative comes from sin. Gossip, curse words, diseases, impure thoughts, bad habits, lying, rage, et cetera, are born from sin. "Well, I don't think everything that is negative is sin." If we still lived in the perfect, yes *perfect*, world God made, there would be no need for distinction between positive or negative. Put another way, there would be no need for a differentiation between good or evil. Have you ever noticed how the beginning of the Bible starts? Let's look together, is that cool? I feel like we are getting to know each other pretty well, and we can just check stuff out together from here on out.

> And God said, "Let there be light," and there was light. God saw that the light was good, and he separated the light from darkness. (Gn 1:3–4 NIV)
>
> And God said, "Let the water under the sky be gathered to one place, and let dry ground appear." And it was so. God called the dry ground "land," and the gathered waters he called "seas." And God saw that it was good.

(Gn 1:9-10 NIV)

Then God said, "Let the land produce vegetation: seed-bearing plants and trees on the land that bear fruit with seed in it, according to their various kinds." And it was so. The land produced vegetation: plants bearing seed according to their kinds and trees bearing fruit with seed in it according to their kinds. And God saw that it was good. (Gn 1:11-12 NIV)

And God said, "Let there be lights in the vault of the sky to separate the day from the night, and let them serve as signs to mark sacred times, and days and years, and let them be lights in the vault of the sky to give light on the earth." And it was so. God made two great lights, the greater light to govern the day and the lesser light to govern the night. He also made the stars. God set them in the vault of the sky to give light on the earth, to govern the day and the night, and to separate light from darkness, And God saw that it was good. (Gn 1:14-18 NIV)

And God said, "Let the water teem with living creatures, and let birds fly above the earth across the vault of the sky." So God created the great creatures of the sea and every living thing with which the water teems and that moves about in it, according to their kinds, and every winged bird according to its kind. And God saw that it was good. (Gn 1:20-21 NIV)

And God said, "Let the land produce living creatures according to their kinds: the livestock, the creatures that move along the ground, and the wild animals, each according to its kind." And it was so. God made the wild animals according to their kinds, the livestock according to their kinds, and all the creatures that move along the ground according to their kinds. And God saw that it was good. (Gn 1:24-25 NIV)

God saw all that he had made, and it was very good. And there was evening, and there was morning—the sixth day. (Gn 1:31 NIV)

Now, did anyone happen to notice the common trait in each of those verses? I'm sure you did. "And God saw that it was good." This is everything to my point. God is always good. He evokes good. He embodies good. He *is* Good! He cannot do anything negative, it is always positive things that He is doing. Notice that none of those verses said, "And God saw that it was pretty good." Or, "And God saw that it was good enough to get the job done." So, if God looked at all he had done and saw that it was "very good," then that means there was no negative in the world. It wasn't until Adam and Eve sinned, disobeying the one rule, that negative came into the world. Side note: sometimes, when I read Genesis and about Adam and Eve, I wanna scream, "You had one job guys!" So it would make sense that God gave us power within our words to be triumphant and command our lives forward and to be prosperous.

I think the enemy knows this to some degree. The Devil is no dummy. He is *The* Great Liar. Learning how to guard our words and always remaining faithful and honest even when it hurts, is the key to our progressing this world into a better place. Now, does that mean we are always going to be perfect, no. No one will ever be perfect like Jesus was or God is, but we can strive everyday to walk as close to the likeness of Jesus as possible. That means speaking life and not death. There's a great passage in the book I mentioned earlier by Francis P. Martin, that deals with something that we do everyday to either ourselves or other people. In the book he mentions that we sometimes speak over our children saying things like, "Oh, Suzie is not good at test taking," or, "Jimmy has just never been that good at math," and even, "Sarah just gets really nervous when it comes to things like this." Talk about not even giving your kids a fighting chance. How often do you say things like this about your children, others' children, or even yourself. I know I have done this myself on several occasions.

I feel like I can hear you saying, "Well, jeez la-weez. I have to pay attention to everything that comes out of my mouth? That's impossible! We use a lot of words everyday." It's not impossible. Will it take time and practice to get a hold on the things that you say? Sure it will. It will be like strengthening a new muscle. But what happens when you exercise a muscle enough? It gets stronger and it doesn't *hurt* so much because you've been strengthening and conditioning it.

I think, if I had to boil it down to one main point for this chapter, it's that Satan is using our habits against us to build himself up in our society. Most of the time it is on a subconscious level that we speak negatives over people, not realizing the Devil is using us! As a matter of fact, this negativity becomes prevalent in our society. Again, think about all the people you know that gossip or speak negatively over situations or people. Has this not become so commonplace within our culture? It's become so common to be in other people's personal lives and business that some of the top pieces of entertainment are reality shows built around drama (*The Real World, Keeping Up with the Kardashians, Real Housewives*). Even a number of magazines are solely built on speculation or conjured up stories about celebrities. In reality, those stories are flat out lies or told at the expense of others. Even when it comes to an individualistic view of ourselves, we need to take inventory. How many of these statements do we speak on a daily basis? How many times have we said, "Oh, I can't do that. I'm not good at communicating with people." Or what about gossiping with your coworkers about other coworkers?

I'll admit that correcting negative speech is not easy to do. Let me say that again. *These are not easy things to correct.* There—now no one is under any disillusion that correcting these habits will be easy. The good news: with help from God and some determination, you can begin to curb, and eventually fix these habits within your daily life. Here's something I've noticed as I've been fixing these habits within my own life. Satan wants to keep you on the path of the unrighteous. It's his way of getting back at God and continuing his rebellion that started long ago. So, when it comes to fixing these issues, I've noticed that it seems like I run into adversity left and right. Now, if you've read any books from faith driven authors, you know that Satan is not omniscient, omnipotent, or omnipresent. He *cannot* be in every place at once like God. However, when he rebelled against God, the Bible says, "His tail swept down a third of the stars of heaven and cast them to the earth. And the dragon stood before the woman who was about to give birth, so that when she bore her child he might devour it," (Rv 12:4 ESV). We don't know how many one-third of the angels is, because we don't know how many angels exist. My guess is it's myriads of angels. The point is, if Satan can't be where you are, then perhaps one of his fallen homies is instead. Perhaps we are given a hint at how many angels exist by likening them to metaphorical stars. How many stars are in the sky at night? If I had to guess I would say it's well over one billion or more. Let's just use 1 billion for our example. A third of one billion is 333,333,333.3 repeating. Since God has known the plan all along, I believe He accounted for what the population would be when the time drew closer for Jesus to return. I think the number of angels in Heaven reflects and accounts for this, and then some. There are a few verses in the Bible that give us a hint as to the number of angels there are, such as, "Then I looked and heard the voice of many angels, numbering thousands upon thousands, and ten thousand times ten thousand," (Rv 5:11 NIV). I know that's not a billion. But, you have to place the writing within the context of the period in which it was written. This may have been a case of the writer not knowing how to aptly express the amount, because the sheer number of angels that were there was not a word that existed in that time. My point is this, there is simply no way that God did not account for needing more than a third of the angels when it came to what the population would eventually become through the course of time. Remember, He is all-knowing. When you start correcting your habits, and you still feel the enemy or his minions coming for you, rest assured that you have protection in the form of God the Father and his host of elect angels.

Spiritual warfare is real and our words pierce like arrows and sharpened steel.

4

Titles Among Men

WHEN PEOPLE THINK ABOUT building up Satan, it comes across as if they think you have to be a part of the occult, or possibly sacrificing cats in a cemetery. Maybe they think you have to be practicing the dark arts, or playing with ouija boards. However, I don't think this is the case. If we look back at the original sin, which was Adam and Eve eating from the tree of knowledge of good and evil, the goal here from Satan's standpoint was, "How can I separate these new beings from God, who I so despise?" Answer? By distracting Adam and Eve.

From what we can tell in the beginning of Genesis, the tree of knowledge of good and evil wasn't some sort of nagging issue with Adam or Eve. It more or less seems that God says, "don't eat from it," and Adam says, "got it!" Now, could it be the case that God told Adam of the tree, then Adam had this nagging curiosity in his mind about why he couldn't eat from the tree? Sure. However, if that were the case, then why does Satan hold such a lengthy conversation with Eve about eating from the tree? A convincing conversation at that, bending the truth just a little to get her to think as Satan wanted her to think. My personal opinion is that neither Adam nor Eve really gave any thought to the tree. They understood they could not eat from it—that was that. Satan purposefully distracts both Adam and Eve with a flat out lie. All in a calculated effort to get them to take their minds, faith, and trust off of God. When the enemy uses distractions, sometimes they are backed by lies, sometimes they are laced with fear and used to nudge you in the opposite direction, and sometimes it's truth used to the enemy's advantage. If we look around our world, what has become the pinnacle of human achievement? I'm not talking about actual events, I'm talking in congruence with feeling and/or knowing, "I've made it!"

Titles. If you look at places like LinkedIn, Bumble Bizz, Shapr, and other career/job related platforms, it's a who's who among who. Now, hopefully we know each other well enough by now that you know I'm not judging. Heck! I use 2 of those 3 platforms to network with individuals and make solid connections for my future endeavours. However, in talking with most people within these sites about life and plans for the future, I've begun to notice something. A good portion of people don't seem to be thinking about the future, or being an active part of their families' futures. They sure aren't thinking about how to begin to heal this great country of ours. Many individuals that I talk to only have one goal, that is to continue working for the company through which they are currently employed, and hopefully getting that next big promotion. Maybe someone can remind me, because I forget sometimes, when they give you big promotions and move you up the corporate ladder, do they usually expect more hours from you, or less? How about more responsibility, or less?

My father is a great man. He gave us a great, *above par*, middle class life. We were not crazy rich, but we also weren't struggling to make ends meet—that I'm aware of. He's also an extremely devout Christian, husband, and father. Although, as he's grown over time, not only in age but perspective as well, we've had a chance to have some great talks about life and purpose. I'll never forget when he told me that he felt he had given too much of himself to his job, and that if he could do it again, he would find a way to spend more uninterrupted time with his family. Like I said, my sister and I had a great life growing up. We never lacked anything we needed,

Titles Among Men

but we also didn't get everything we wanted. A lot of what made growing up so great were the trips we took. My parents enjoyed taking us to do things they viewed as family oriented. Things like skiing, camping at the great Garner State Park, beaches, and a trip to Hawaii. Skiing was probably my favorite, after Hawaii of course. That's where I learned to snowboard, and I've been a board-sports guy ever since.

Unfortunately though, at times I remember my dad having to stop to take a phone call with a peer at the plant or to speak to higher administration about current issues at the work site. At times, I felt like I was getting half a fatherly experience. And those were just the trips. A good portion of time at home was also dedicated to *after hours* work or phone calls. Now, my next question to you is: do you think this is what God intended for us after the events of the garden? Do you think He was like, "I really hope that people work jobs that demand so much from them that they can hardly spend time with their families or spend time with me so I can help them find their true purposes." I'm gonna go ahead and go out on a limb here and say, I don't believe that's what He wanted for us. It seems as though our culture these days has become very wrapped up in status. For instance, what school did you attend, how many degrees and titles do you have to your name, or what sort of success have you made for yourself?

Let's pause a little before I continue, because when you start talking about purpose and goals, sometimes, people can get a little upset or downright offended. "So, I can't chase my goals and dreams? I can't work for the dream company I've always wanted to work for?" That's not what I am saying at all! It's good to have goals and dreams and desires. It's great that you want to work for a company that you feel holds similar values as yourself. It's great, too, that you want to make more money, so your kids won't struggle like you did when you were growing up.

God wants us to have the desires of our hearts. "Delight yourself in the Lord, and He will give you the desires of your heart," (Ps 37:4 NKJV). Delight yourself in the Lord and He will give you what you want. Some people hear or read that and try to reason it out in a logical humanistic way. "Well, if God truly loved me, He would give me what I want, no matter what. I shouldn't have to praise Him or believe in Him. If He's as *living* as people say He is, then why is there a stipulation to getting what I want? That doesn't seem loving." It's funny to me when I hear people reason out God's ways, and it accurately reflects how we handle things here on Earth sometimes.

How many of you have kids, a best friend, or maybe a really great coworker that you enjoy hanging out with? Now, imagine that you have incredible amounts of wealth. You never have to borrow from banks, you pay cash for things so you can steer clear of debt and you provide for your community when needed. Now, imagine your child grows up and moves away, your best friend gets transferred to another state for a job, or that coworker moves departments to another floor of the building. In all of those situations, none of the individuals keep in contact with you. In fact, you are always the one reaching out to set up a friendly rendezvous. These colleagues don't seem to have time to keep in touch. However, every time they need money, they come to you. Any time they need a glowing recommendation, they come to you. Any time they need your help, because they feel a little out of their league, they come to you. Do you think that would get old? Do you think you would get upset and frustrated? Do you think that you might not answer the phone when you see it's them? Simply because you know, without a shadow of doubt, that they need or want something, and aren't just calling to see how you're doing? Why do you feel that way? Is it because it makes you feel as though you are nothing more than a *means to an end* with them, a way to help them get what they want? That it makes you question whether they care about you as much as you care about them? Last question. Do you think *God* could feel that way sometimes? I believe He can. He's not some robot without feelings. "And Jesus went forth, and saw a great multitude, and was moved with compassion toward them, and He healed their sick," (Mt 14:14 NKJV).

Jesus was the earthly human form of God. Jesus is the way God chose to show us who He was when He was among us. If

God had been without feelings, then things like sickness, death, or even the emotions of people He met while on Earth wouldn't have caused any sort of reaction from Him. That's not the case though. He did, and does have feelings. He loves us. He only wants to bring good into our lives. All we need to do is stay in touch with Him, talk to Him, pray, and read His word. It's the same with the goals and dreams you're chasing. If you don't read the Bible with frequency, seek him in prayer, or associate with other Christians, and all you do is ask and ask and ask, then, why would the Lord want to give you anything at all? Of course, one of the great things about God is that He does not hold grudges, act in ways that are childish, or ignore you. If you have accepted Him into your heart, then He is more than happy to welcome you with open arms when you begin seeking Him again in life. Again, I'm speaking from experience.

Alright, let's get back to our regularly scheduled program. We were talking about *titles* of people, what they *do*. Our world has become so obsessed with this idea that it has created division, not unity. I had the opportunity to read a really great book that shed some light on why this division exists, why we have created an institution that hands out titles based on knowledge learned within the walls of these institutions.

The book is *Outwitting the Devil*, by Napoleon Hill. If you haven't read it, I would encourage you to do so if learning different perspectives is your thing. If you already believe you know it all, then maybe not. This book has had an interesting journey from being written to published. It was originally written in 1938 by Napoleon Hill and subsequently locked away for some 73 years before being published in June of 2011. Why so long? According to Hill's family, Hill, himself, was uncertain as to how the public might react to the book and its strong viewpoints. In the book, our titular character, Hill, has an apparent conversation with the Devil. Using his time wisely while he has the attention of the Lord of Darkness, he asks questions about the Devil's work around us on a daily basis. The entirety of the book is an incredibly interesting read, but one part in particular grabbed my utmost attention. The chapter is titled, "Education and Religion." In this chapter, Hill converses with the Devil on just how the Devil affects religious institutions as well as academia. Here's a brief excerpt from this chapter:

> Question: Is that all that is wrong with the system?
>
> Answer (the Devil): No, that is only the beginning. Another major weakness of the school system is that it does not establish in the minds of children either the importance of definiteness of purpose or make any attempt to teach youths how to be definite about anything. The major object of schooling is to force the students to cram their memories with facts instead of teaching them how to organize and make practical use of facts. This cramming system centers the attention of students on the accumulation of "credits" but overlooks the important question of how to use knowledge in the practical affairs of life. This system turns out graduates whose names are inscribed upon parchment certificates, but whose minds are empty of self-determination. The school system got off to a bad start at the beginning. The schools began as institutions of "higher learning," operated entirely for the select few whose wealth and family entitled them to education. Thus, the entire school system was evolved by beginning at the top and working back down to the bottom. It is no wonder the system neglects to teach children the importance of definiteness of purpose when the system, itself, has literally evolved through indefiniteness. (172–3)

I understand why Mr. Hill kept this book to himself for so long. The views expressed in this small excerpt are pretty strong. However, I can't help but think that a good portion of teachers feel this way today. I am currently a teacher, and I know for a fact this is how I feel about the school system. We have slowly but surely bled out any thoughtful conversations, curriculum, or mindsets within our school system in the 21st century.

The Devil has manipulated the school system to get people to forget about the important questions of how to use knowledge in life. We don't even give the next generation the option to learn self-help topics. Want to learn about spirituality or religion? Nope. Want to learn about how to create financial independence for your family? Nope. Want to learn how to stay focused on your goals, speak over your life, and have definiteness of purpose and drive? Nope. You won't find this training in the public education system. We just ask questions like, "What do you want to do when you grow up?" Then we wonder why, by the time they are in middle school, they feel as though they don't have direction or feel as if they have no worth. "Well, I think you're exaggerating a bit with that statement, Jeremy. I don't think students necessarily feel that way." Bet me! I've taught some. I've had conversations around it. A lot of the kids I teach come from poor backgrounds. Some of them have a genuine desire to help others in their same situation. Unfortunately, we never teach the next generation how to make that happen. Nope! Can't do that. Really, it doesn't seem like a *can't* these days, it seems like a *won't*. We would rather bathe our children in mediocrity than help them to go as high and as far as they can in this world. And that is where we arrive at this idea of titles.

Make sure you have a great title so everyone knows you're important. Make sure you have a good title so people know they're not more important than you. Care to take a peek behind the curtain? To see how many of those title holders are actually happy and fulfilled? How many children of *successful people* feel neglected and forgotten? How many wives feel the same as well? How many of those people wonder, "Is this it? Is this what it was all for?" Do you think that it's coincidental that the top three to five regrets people have when faced with the end of life has to do with being happy, being true to themselves, or spending too much time at their job? I don't. I think that as people begin to near the end of their time, they think retrospectively about life. If we think about Satan and his ultimate goal to thwart God, which includes lying and manipulation, would it be too far-fetched to think that, maybe at the end, he says, "Here, see for yourself. Gotcha! Look at how much time you've wasted. Look at how far you've pushed your children away from you. Look at how many people you could have helped but didn't because I kept your mind full of a selfish, self-serving attitude. Look at the example I was able to instill in your kids so that they follow the same path and stay far away from God and their own families. Surely I have pulled a fast one on you. Ha!"

But surely he hasn't pulled a fast one on us. Even in our waning hours of life, we can still reach out to our Heavenly Father and ask him to come into our hearts and forgive us of a life of sin and selfishness. Even when the Devil thinks he's won, he hasn't.

> Two other men, both criminals, were also led out with him to be executed. When they came to the place called the Skull, they crucified him there, along with the criminals—one on his right, the other on his left... One of the criminals who hung there hurled insults at him: Aren't you the Messiah? Save yourself and us! But the other criminal rebuked him. "Don't you fear God," he said, "since you are under the same sentence? We are punished justly, for we are getting what our deeds deserve. But this man has done nothing wrong. Then he said, "Jesus, remember me when you come into your kingdom." Jesus answered him, "truly I tell you, today you will be with me in paradise." (Lk 23:32 & 39-43 NIV)

If you think I am off-base with this thought, I would encourage you to do the due diligence and start having conversations with people, asking them if they are really feeling fulfilled these days. Are they getting the amount of time with their kids they want? Are they able to help their parents like they want? Are they able to give to charities and be as philanthropic as they would like to be? Are they experiencing *joy* in their life?

Joy and happiness are two different things. *Happiness* can be affected by this world in which we live, through the daily frictions and heartaches we experience. *Joy* comes from the Lord, and allows you to experience the world in a completely different way. You may say, "I just don't think there's a distinction between joy and happiness. I think they're both the same." Consider this example. Everyday at my school, there is a custodian who, no matter what he's doing, is always singing old spanish songs that he knows.

How many educated and refined individuals do you know would be singing if they had to do hard manual labor like buffing and mopping floors, or cleaning bathrooms? Middle school bathrooms at that! I'll be honest, I don't think my attitude would be on point to muster up that kind of joy while doing that sort of work. That tells me I need to work on my joy. That's a great example of someone who lives a joyous life, not just a happy one.

If you feel like you're no longer fulfilled, or maybe you are finding yourself irritable these days, and it's more noticeable when you're at work, then maybe you should start digging into and asking questions around your purpose. Ask yourself, "How is it that I am wanting to live?" or "What do I want my life to look like?" Instead of just repeating "What else do I want to do?" Don't let this world or the Devil falsely convince you that if you're not going to college or working a specific career path, then you're not a person of value. We all have value. God has a bigger purpose for us. He knew the plans he had for us before we were ever born. "'For I know the plans I have for you,' declares the Lord, 'plans to prosper you and not to harm you, plans to give you hope and a future,'" (Jer 29:11 NIV).

5

Self-Gratification

IF YOU HOP ON the interwebs and search for *The most beautiful places on Earth*, you'll be inundated with pictures from across the globe of beautiful landscapes, awe-inspiring vegetation, animals, cultural scenes, and environments. This world is so vast, large, and brilliant in its design. There are many places to see and experience. Sometimes, I think about this world, and find myself amazed and astonished at how many places there are to visit, cultures to experience, and sites to see. For the individual, this can either be a blessing or a curse.

The human race has been blessed with the gift of thought and ideas. We are able to make anything from beautiful sculptures, to incredibly fast cars, to powerful weapons. I'm amazed by some of the things that great minds have invented. Unfortunately, any of this can be used by the Devil to seduce us into drifting further and further away from God. No, I don't think all inventions are for the sole purpose of corrupting mankind. However, I do think that good men can be corrupted along the way if they allow it. The Devil is very devious and convincing. He slyly makes man think he is the one accomplishing innovation and making this world better without the help of God. When that happens, the innovation taints and deepens the growing rift between man and God. And

SELF-GRATIFICATION

for what? It is usually for the sake of prospering the individual, to secure for themselves the riches of the world so that they may live a comfortable life with all the possessions they desire. After all, if God isn't making me wealthy fast enough, then I, man, will make sure it happens as quickly as I can. This leaves God out of the picture.

Let me clarify this statement. I do not think that it's bad to want more for yourself and your family. If you have desires to own a fast car or a yacht, a mansion or a fleet of motorcycles with a garage built to hold them, I don't think that's bad. Let's point to that scripture from earlier once again, "Delight yourself in the Lord, and he will give you the desires of your heart," (Ps 37:4 NKJV). The Lord our God wants us to be happy and live an abundant life. That's abundance in all things: health, wealth, marriage, employment, etc. He knows that having things can make us happy—to a certain degree. It is only when we become too attached to worldly possessions that we begin to find ourselves in danger of placing possessions over God.

As a youth, I remember hearing sermons about "money being the root of all evil." The only problem with that statement is that, usually, people leave out the beginning of that scripture. "For the love of money is the root of all kinds of evil. And some people, craving money, have wandered from the true faith and pierced themselves with many sorrows," (1 Tm 6:10 NLT). Read that again so you can make sure you understand what is being said, I'll wait.

Elevator music

The topic is the *love* of money. The pastors and preachers of my youth failed to completely explain this to me. These days, it does seem like a good amount of pastors have become better at talking about success and the money that comes with it, and how to keep your trust and faith bound to God and not money. Nevertheless, when I was younger, and in a different time, that's not how it was approached. As I understood it, their sermons led me to believe that the accumulation of wealth was wrong. Money, in itself, was demonized from the standpoint that no good could come from it. Those who had it were bad, evil, and vile people who would do anything to keep their riches intact. Does that mean that all wealthy people are pure and good, of course not. My point is, from a young age I was already basically being told, "If you try to have a lot of money, then you are far from God." As scripture says, it is only when we become obsessed with money, desiring it more than our relationship with our Heavenly Father, that we have "wandered from the true faith and pierced [ourselves] with many sorrows." And yet we still demonize money in our culture and in our families. I understand that the use of *demonize* here is a strong word, but I do believe that we have gone to great lengths in our world to downplay money and how it can be used for good. Look at how many in the latest generation think capitalism is wrong, and yet they shop at big-box stores and sip iced coffees. Perhaps, it is the underlying philosophy of the corporation and the ones in charge, not the capitalistic framework.

Before I move on to another pertinent piece of scripture or two, I would like to ask you a question. No, not another rhetorical question like those I've asked thus far. An actual question that I want you to answer out loud, wherever you may be. Ready? Here's the question: Do you think there is a way for society to better prepare people for acquiring a lot of money, and to show them how to do good with it? If you answered *no*, then I would suggest reflecting on why you said no. Take a good look at yourself, be introspective. You can't project your intentions onto the unborn. If you answered *yes*, then you are in good company! There are plenty of others out there in the world that think as you do, and they are making themselves known. I'm talking about the Robert Kiosakis and Gary Vaynerchuks of the world. People who have made it their mission to fill in the gaps within the educational system that, in my opinion, have been purposefully left out. I especially like Gary Vee's thought process on helping the next generation. He calls it *Capitalism 2.0: the acquisition of wealth*. It's not about just *getting mine*. It's about *getting mine* and then turning around and helping others get theirs, while also teaching respect and longterm mentality. When we think about preparing people to be good stewards

Self-Gratification

of their money, we need to first look at where we are potentially dropping the ball. Demonizing money does nothing to help society learn how to handle money. If anything, we encourage people to remain *average* and never set, or chase after goals.

Another area that needs consideration is our school system. We do nothing to prepare our children for wealth, or teach them any guiding principles surrounding wealth management and mentality. We push them along in the educational system, only encouraging them to excel academically. Which, for those few who do want to excel in academia, great! But, what of those who at the end of the required 12 years of school, are given a diploma and released into society as young adults looking to create something more for themselves or their families? The school system didn't prepare them for that, it created employees. Now, if they have any ingenuity, some may become sole proprietors or small business owners. At the *extreme*, the best few will go on to be investors, moguls, and brilliant entrepreneurs. Most will continue the struggle of working mediocre jobs just to exist in this world with no real understanding of how to manage their money.

We do not talk about *all* the different ways to make money in this country in school. Have you ever wondered why the 52-year-old couple that wins the mega-jackpot lottery goes broke not long after? According to an article published by CNBC in 2017, "Lottery winners are more likely to declare bankruptcy within three to five years than the average American. What's more, studies have shown that winning the lottery does not necessarily make you happier or healthier." Why do these individuals go bankrupt? Because they were never taught how to manage money well. They were never given the mindset around having a lot of money. I personally believe that they did not rely on the Lord their God to guide them on just how to use the money, either.

I want to look at two scriptures now that I was going to mention before. Here's what our wonderful Creator says about wealth and riches: "'Bring all the tithes into the storehouse so there will be enough food in my Temple. If you do,' says the Lord of Heaven's Armies, 'I will open the windows of heaven for you. I will pour out a blessing so great you won't have enough room to take it in. Try it! Put me to the test!'" (Mal 3:10 NLT).

Crickets Crickets

Anybody else feeling like that's a God that doesn't want us to have plenty? Not only does he say that he will pour out blessings for us, but on top of that, the Big G says, "Try me. Test my words!" That's a stark difference from the pastor at the pulpit staring you down on Sunday morning saying, "Money is bad! Money turns good men evil!" Money doesn't turn men evil. People allow the Devil to convince them that they need more and more wealth. The love of money is the just conduit through which the Devil works. That's just like the old saying, "Guns kill people." No, people kill people, it's just sometimes they use a gun, knife, rope, water, shovel, or scissors.

You might be saying, "Okay, he wants to give me blessings, but I've been working hard all my life, and I still don't see any blessings!" Look at the start of the scripture. "Bring all the tithes ... " What's a tithe? "One-tenth of the produce of the land, whether grain from the fields or fruit from the trees, belongs to the Lord and must be set apart to him as holy," (Lv 27:30 NLT). Ten percent of what you make from your job, that gig you played, the side hustle you have going on, or the lawns you mow belongs to God. "Well, where or who do I give this ten percent to?" The scripture says, "in my Temple." This referred to the actual temple where the Hebrews went to worship. Today, it would be a local church where you attend and hold membership.

"Nope! Nope! Nope! Not gonna do it! I've read too many stories about churches using funds inappropriately and scamming the congregation. I just won't do that!" Do you believe that every church out there is bad? That among the 384,000 congregations, according to a paper published by *Journal for the Scientific Study of Religion* in 2017, that all of them are bad? Find a local church you believe won't spend your tithe inappropriately. Ask them what needs to be done to join the committee that makes decisions on where tithing is spent. Ask them out right where the tithing goes and if they have somewhere you can visibly see where the money is going, like a website, cause, or newsletter addressing monthly expenditures. "I can't do that." Why not? If you're concerned about where possible tithings go, then you have every right to ask. If they can't answer those questions or won't, then maybe that's not the church for you. Go find another one. "What if I go through a lot of churches that say that?" Then you'll go through a lot of churches. Don't let laziness be the reason you don't give to God what is owed him and in the process, block riches from yourself. Some church somewhere will be glad to tell you where the money goes. Heck! They might even take you to the office and crack open the books for you to see for yourself! People with nothing to hide don't mind showing you what others keep hidden. If anything, I would take it as a sign that the church is doing its part to use the money they receive for the glory of God.

Good people are persuaded by the lure of money all the time by the Devil. Do you think God is going to say, "Oh you know what? That church you gave to didn't spend the money appropriately, so that deal I have with you is actually . . . null and void. Sorry." A promise from God is a covenant to be counted and relied upon. You can take that to the bank!

By now you have hopefully developed a good feel for my writing style. I start with an idea and then dive in from behind instead of head on. I always pray that God guides my thoughts and my fingers as I type this book. I'd like to take the position of deconstructing the process to understand what led us to the original presented idea. So, what was the original idea here? That we, in essence, unknowingly give more credit to Satan when we focus much of our lives on the acquisition of material things. However, to understand why we fall prey to doing this, we had to look at two incredibly influential institutions.

The first was the church and the second was education. By preaching that money is the root of all evil, we fail to shed light upon the fact that God wants us to have the desires of our heart and to be prosperous. After all, it's the *love of money* that is bad, not money itself. We miss a great opportunity to teach the younger generation about how to use money as a tool to help impoverished people. Instead, people can wind up resolving themselves to a lifestyle where they work hard for the money they make and judge others that have more; they begin to seeth with envy towards those that they perceive as having a more fulfilling lifestyle because of the money they possess. Remember, money won't fulfill you in the long run. It can only alleviate the stress you may feel around your personal finances. Money will never give you your purpose. Only God can do that.

Rather than taking the pulpit approach, our schools do something equally as destructive but from a position that is guised as *improvement*. We usually talk about money in terms of what you do when you grow up and the career that you aspire to obtain. We do not go over the different methods in which you can create income or monies for yourself in this country. Why? I believe it was a plan set in motion long ago by Satan himself, with God's permission (see Erwin Lutzer's book, *God's Devil*, if you don't understand what I mean), to bottleneck the amount of influence from individuals. "Huh? I'm lost. What do you mean?" The raw reality of it is, money gains you influence. You've heard the cliche statement, *money talks*. The more money you have, the more people will listen to you, regardless of whether you know anything about a subject or not. They will listen! "Well, I don't think that's the way it should be." I agree. However, I once heard someone say, "There's a world that is and a world that should be. Unfortunately we live in the world that is." The quicker you come to terms with that, the quicker, in my opinion, you can start moving ahead. We will talk about moving ahead in the next chapter.

Our influence gives us a chance to speak into others' lives, and, with the help of the Holy Spirit, help them along in the journey of life. We know this idea to be sound, because if we think of two people walking up to an important event on a topic they care about, and one says, "I'm pretty well known around here, and I have an impeccable character. I'd like to take a few minutes to speak." The other says, "I've got a four million dollar check and the funds verification on my phone to prove it, ready to go to your cause. I'd like to take a moment and speak." What are the odds that person number one will get the slot to speak over number two? I'm not saying money makes you better. What I'm saying is money gives you a platform in which to speak about causes, purpose, and belief. Whether your heart is bolstered in good or bad—unfortunately.

So, if we look at how the idea of schooling came to be in the first place, which I pointed out earlier in this book, then is it too hard to think that from the beginning, morally corrupt people wanted to ensure that those deemed *beneath them* would never get the chance to have that influence? To keep things more in line with the *status-quo*? I mean, just look at history. How long have we kept the idea in place of kings and queens, emperors, and royalty at the top and the rest at the bottom? Do you think that when the kings of old heard that other, potentially poorer individuals, were beginning to amass more wealth than them and not from a lineage of royalty they said, "Splendid! Invite them to dinner! Let us dine as equals and share in each other's knowledge and accomplishments!" Something in my gut tells me this is not what happened. It is because of this reason we need to, now more than ever, help our future generations to turn from the lifestyles of excess they see without proper context (Instagram) and show them how to not only gain the stability they seek for their families, but also to help so many others.

We need to stop breeding an *I* mentality in regards to one's purpose and the impact on others. "*I* love what *I* do. *My* job fulfills *me*." What about all the other people that need you out there, who can't follow your exact path? The one thing we all have the ability to do is become better. Notice I didn't say smarter. I said, *better*. Grow yourself in faith, in empathy and relating to people, in seeking perspective and insight from people placed in your life that have wisdom and soundness of mind. I think many great minds, regardless if they shared a relationship with God, have proven that you can become of significance in this world without continuing to higher education. I believe that we can achieve that position in life. However, we need God's help to maintain and see the responsibilities through.

Your Devil Is Too Big

". . . When someone has been given much, much will be required in return; and when someone has been entrusted with much even more will be required," (Lk 12:48 NLT).

6

A World Against

AS A REMINDER, I began the previous chapter with the purpose of this book. Each of the ideas that I have outlined in these chapters are things that I think we have done to build up the Devil in our society, things that make him seem larger than life. Some of the ideas are very straightforward in their explanation. Others come from the vantage point of habits or societal norms that encourage us to think that the Devil must be alive and well and so powerful, because look at all these bad things people do on a daily basis. These topics are not meant to be definitive. These topics are meant to serve as a way to get you thinking about the possible ways that we potentially spread the larger than life portrait of Satan, whether it be intentional or unintentional. Mostly, people don't think about Satan's presence in our daily lives. However, the individuals that inherit even our unintentional ideologies are mostly in our immediate families, not the world at large. That, to me, is more dangerous because you are instilling beliefs and ideologies into your family lineage. If you know anything about how hard generational mindsets are to adjust or correct, such as a poverty mindset, then that is the last thing you want to leave behind.

With that said, let's move on to our next topic. Teaching preteen and teen kids for the last 5 years, I've grown used to a familiar phrase. "It's because *xyz* doesn't like me." Or sometimes, "It's because he/she hates me." You may also be familiar with this comment as it seems as though our world loves to say this frequently, "This race of people doesn't like us! Positions of authority don't like us! This religion has it out for us! This country doesn't want us! Democrats have it out for us! Republicans have it out for us! The government as a whole has it out for us!" Want me to sum up what they are all saying a little bit better? "This world is out to get *me*!" This, unfortunately, is the mindset that a good portion of America has, and, quite possibly, the world (notice I said *possibly*). Nothing ever works *in* their favor because things don't work *to* their favor. This sort of ideology is running rampant in our society. When we use this phrase, or come at life from the standpoint that *the world is against me*, in my opinion, we run the real risk of insinuating two things:

1. God doesn't care about us.
2. The Devil is more powerful than God.

On the one hand, if the world's against us, who made the world? God! So that statement begins to morph into "God is against me." If that's the way we begin to look at it or perceive it, then we start to paint the enemy in a light he does not deserve. If we go the other direction and say that this world surely has been overcome by the Devil, and nothing will save us, we are giving too much credit where none is deserved. Truly, the only thing that can save us is the Savior. Even if these were just statements we thought to ourselves, that is where Satan prefers to meet us in battle. Left to our own devices, we succumb to them. The enemy wants nothing more than to overtake our minds and fully convince us that he is more powerful than God, and that he rules over all mankind.

The real problem lies in the fact that we do not keep these ideas to ourselves. We include others in our *woes*. We rally the troops! We send out the call to arms! We invite people in and encourage them to stay in our misery and self-deprivation. It's no wonder that there are so many individuals out there that consistently blame others for their problems. It's always everyone else's fault for why their life is the way it is. They even include God in the fault finding! Even the most spiritually driven person can walk into the snare laid by the enemy and allow themselves to become a victim. If that isn't enough, some individuals are passing this mentality down to their kids, who in turn pass it on to theirs, and so forth. For this reason, we need to be careful to speak positively, not negatively, over those in our realm of influence. No, this requires more action on our parts. It requires a resolute decision to be more careful how we speak and to whom we speak. God blessed humans with an incredible spirit and a will to conquer even the most dire of circumstances. God does allow you to sometimes experience circumstances the Devil has placed in your path as a way to strengthen you. "Well, I just can't believe God would do that. He loves us! He could not be a caring, loving God if He let bad situations and things happen to us!"

Really? When you were learning to walk as a baby, were your parents always around ready to catch you? Did they follow you around with a pillow, so just in case you fell, you would land on a nice cushy surface? Most likely, this was not the case. They let you fall. Why? Because you would never have developed the ability to persist with learning to walk. On the other hand, perhaps you would have grown a tendency to hypochondria when taking a tumble. I know that those things can and do certainly happen. No, I'm not a doctor. What I do know from being in education and around children for 12 years, getting to see the different ways that parents handle adversity, I can say that I have personally seen these two examples in action.

The student who doesn't know how to push through adversity or a tough situation, because mom or dad is always there to intervene, will not develop the tenacity to overcome any kind of adversity. What about the student who falls down, gets a tiny cut, and starts freaking out, convinced that it will get infected if they don't get ER-level care, or frantically runs to the nurse as if they may lose enough blood to potentially need a donor! This student hasn't learned to overcome, or at best, remain level headed during the everyday situations of life.

Your Devil Is Too Big

I know that as a parent, you feel it's your job to help your child through life in those early years, and hopefully they will come back and still seek your advice in their later years. We cannot continue to coddle and make excuses for why things happen to our children. It's not always someone else's fault. Perhaps it would help them to know that God is using the situation, not to punish us, but to make us stronger. He will bring good out of the adverse situation. We should be explaining this to our younger generations as one more resource in their tool belt when tough times occur. This is not so as to overload them, but to give them the appropriate thinking tools to call upon in times of adversity.

My dad is a master-class in woodworking and building things. He's built 2 houses from the ground up, multiple decks, wheelchair ramps, patios, pergolas, and so many other things. He even learned to carve wooden ducks. I would watch him as a kid and note things that he did as he taught me along the way. As a kid, I was pretty hyper. I had ADHD, and it was all I could do to sit still or pay attention and focus when something was being taught. However, now that I'm older and have a wife and a house of my own, all of those things he taught me, during those times when I could sit still, are part of my ability to problem solve. I feel pretty confident when doing handyman fixes or building my wife something she saw on Tik Tok or Pinterest. Do I still have to call my dad every once in a while and ask a question to make sure I understand what I am doing? Of course, I do. For the most part though, I can do it on my own because my dad helped me develop my critical thinking and problem solving abilities in this area.

We can do the same thing for our kids in the spiritual arena as well. By equipping our kids, we can effectively help them later in life when the world's hardships happen. If we look at our hardship as being a way that God is strengthening us, then things get way more exciting. Instead of it being a hardship for the sake of hardship, it's a hardship that will prosper us in the end! Praise God! That means, we will grow and change for the better in the end. Is that not something to be excited about? This doesn't mean that God is behind every hardship. The world is still the world, and things happen. We have to live in this messed up world, but we don't have to be like this world. God is *not* constantly trying to test you through adversity. He just uses the circumstances you are in to teach you. His plans for you are to prosper you. Give Him some credit! Still, it doesn't hurt to have a well supplied utility belt. (Had to get a Batman reference in there. *Boom!*)

Look at all the people that God used in a powerful way after using hardship to better refine them. Joseph was thrown down a well and sold into slavery by his own brothers! He was purchased by a very influential man who put him in charge of many things in his own household. Joseph was framed and wrongfully imprisoned for many years. He was eventually released when God used him to interpret the Pharaoh's dreams. Joseph was placed as the second in command behind the Pharaoh of Egypt. Through all the adversity he endured, he kept his faith in God, and God rewarded him.

Or how about Noah? He was told first hand, by God, that the earth would flood and he should build a very large boat. Even though it hadn't rained in years, or ever, depending on your viewpoint, and the people had all but given up on believing in God, Noah did as God commanded. Noah even had the pleasure of people coming out to ridicule him while he built this large seafaring vessel. That's a hardship for sure! People telling you that you're a crazy person, even though you were told, direct line, that you should definitely build this boat. Each of these men were refined by hardship, not of their making, but used by God to do great things.

The Bible also documents stories of how God used women in mighty ways. Mary's journey to birthing the Savior of the world was not easy. Eventually, she even has to watch as her firstborn son is crucified! Rajab, a prostitute, gave shelter to two angels who had come to destroy the vile city in which she lived. God spared her and her whole family as a result of her faith and obedience. How about Queen Esther? Her story is incredible! She was taken from her normal life to be in the King's harem. Years later, after he has chosen her as queen, she is able to save the entire Hebrew nation. All of these people were refined by hardship, and in the end, blessed by God and were better, stronger, and wiser for it. Imagine if instead of our children saying, "this is God's fault," they might come to say, "this is God's gift!" *Refinement*!

7

Your Future is a Circle

WHEN I FIRST GOT the impulse to write this book, which I feel was inspired by the Holy Spirit, I was unsure if I would initially write on the following topic. It's not because I think the topic isn't worth talking about, but simply because it has been discussed in detail in many other books ad nauseum. However, I did include it due to the fact that all good things are worth repeating. Even the Bible repeats the same truisms from different perspectives, as in Matthew, Mark, Luke, and John. Good things are worth repeating. How many times did you hear the same things growing up, or at least things that were very similar in nature? If you had anyone parenting you when you were young, the answer is: *a lot*. I also thought that the repetition would give credence to the idea for this book. That is, we perpetuate and create the larger than life status given to Lucifer in our current age. Sometimes our efforts are blatantly obvious in things like our media, and sometimes they are more subconscious, like in our habits, thought processes, and our family ideologies.

In my case, something that my parents and teachers told me repeatedly was to be careful who you hang out with and to choose friends carefully. I have, from time to time, found myself telling my own students the same tried and true message. We can see this lesson reflected in people's lives again and again. The interview with the inmate serving a life sentence for murder, recounting how it all began, usually with a gang of unscrupulous characters and bad influences. If backed against a corner, most students will finally admit that others were involved in the vandalism of the school bathroom, and not just them. They just went along with it. We tend to think that the kids who grow up and go on to have successful lives, careers, and influence, listened to the sage advice of their parents and teachers. That they chose their friends and those that surround them carefully. This is known as their *sphere* or *circle of influence*. Sorry to be the bearer of bad news, but in most instances, that just isn't the case.

In the process of growing up and continuing through life, we either become confident in our ability to make good choices, or our self image is too low to be resistant to others' opinions or influence. They do call it your *sphere of influence* for a reason. Once we've matured to adulthood and begin to settle into new job roles, find that new group of progressive friends on campus or even in the recent church congregation we've joined, we start to forget that advice that we once held dear. Since we are now adults, we must know what, and who, is best for us. We no longer think the repeated warning about social association applies. We slowly allow the shadow to befall us, making associations with whomever will allow us friendship. Satan is at work. This will most often result in having friends that aren't the most desirable. If you question their motives, consistently disagree with what they are saying, or the relationship lacks the openness to be yourself with your own views and outlooks, then perhaps you should reconsider your social circle. That's not to say that I don't have *friends* at work, or even acquaintances through life, but I make sure to guard my mind and my time with them. Satan can disguise himself to appeal to your need for friendship. Just accepting and becoming a part of the group can shade us from God's light of wisdom and understanding.

Some of you might be thinking, "But, I know I can trust my friends, family, and a select few coworkers. They would never steer me wrong." Have you actually tested this out? Are you 100% sure and unequivocal in this statement? Here's my personal opinion, and we will also look at what the Bible says about the topic. I think that if God can test us from time to time throughout our lifespan, then we too can test things and people along the way. "I don't test my friends. By choosing to test them it shows that I never really trusted them from the beginning." Sorry, but I'm not sorry to disagree. That's a completely awful mindset to have when it comes to the people with whom you will ultimately spend the majority of your time. We do learn from past experiences and try to apply these learned behaviors to future associations. However, when it's an inconvenient truth that we face, we ignore history in favor of someone else's opinions and viewpoints. What does that have to do with your personal circle?

Look at some of history's most infamous *groups* of people that chose to adhere more to a *hive mind* than actually remaining aware: Hitler and the Nazis, Jim Jones and Jones Town, Charles Manson and the Manson Family, and David Koresh and the Branch Davidians to name a few. The list goes on. Don't you think that maybe someone in the group questioned the leaders motives? Don't you think that for the sake of being a part of the group, some of them just went along with what the leader was telling them? "My friends and I are Nazis? That's a bit extreme." I agree. Those are extreme examples. Look past the extremes to the correlation I made. What do they all share in common? No one stopped to question or challenge by saying, "Hey, should we really think this way? Do these beliefs advocate for such causes?" One could argue that no one asked because they were too scared of the repercussions for asking, and maybe that is true. However, we should never let fear be our excuse to avoid asking tough questions, dive deeper into a hard topic, or talk about uncomfortable ideologies. This is partly why the world is where it is today.

Too many people are concerned with tarnishing a relationship, being excluded from the group, or losing that title they worked so hard for, instead of bringing up the hard questions or topics. So, what do I mean when I say *test*? Firstly, it's not an "Aha!

Gotcha!" moment. Comments such as those are divisive and create distance. Secondly, it's a moment when your spirit is quickened to express how you truly feel about a subject. If those in the group are true friends, your differences won't separate you. They should bring you closer together. Why? Because you are starting to understand each other on a deeper, more intimate level.

The friendships and relationships I look for these days are the ones that not only challenge my thinking on different topics, but also the ones where we can disagree and still remain friends. Disagreeing does not mean we hate each other. Being friends does not mean we have to see each other all the time or think alike all the time. It means, when we are together, we enjoy the company, the discussion, the intimacy, and the freedom to be ourselves. One of my favorite books, *The Art of War* by Sun Tzu, says, "If you know your enemy and know yourself, then you need not fear the result of a hundred battles." So, who is the enemy in these situations? Not each other. It is the one who seeks to destroy relationships—the Devil.

Before diving into why this issue is of such importance and the subconscious implications it has in the world, let's look at what the Bible has to say on this matter. "Don't be fooled by such things, for *bad company corrupts good character*," (1 Cor 15:33 NLT). "Don't team up with those who are unbelievers. How can righteousness be a partner with wickedness? How can light live with darkness?" (2 Cor 6:14 NLT). Now to be clear, I do not think that the Bible is saying that you cannot be friends with or, at times, be around unbelievers. After all, Jesus primarily visited with those considered undesirable in their time period, such as tax collectors, prostitutes, and other sinners. But Jesus wasn't partying it up with these individuals or spending copious amounts of time with them. I think these verses are here to remind us not to allow ourselves to overstay our visit with non-believers—or *bad company*, as the Bible puts it. This is where our old nemesis the Devil comes into play. Always roaming and looking for a place to cause distractions or separate us from God in some way. Sometimes it's the Devil's minions doing his bidding, not him directly.

Your Future is a Circle

When we find that special group of people, that *close-friends* circle, or the coworker happy hour hangout group, are we paying close attention to what is being accomplished during those times? I do not believe that God gave us life, for us to waste time drinking ourselves to confusion, gossiping, complaining, using social media, or streaming videos for hours upon hours.

I believe that God gave us life with purpose. One of our purposes is, and always will be, to help one another to see the light in the darkness of this world, to be encouragers and doers of this world, and to spread the good news of what Jesus Christ did for us on the cross. Jesus gave His life for us so that all we need to do is believe and have faith in Him, then we can be with Him in His kingdom forever. God knew what He had created when He created man and woman. He knew all the potential inside of us. The potential to overcome and our ability to resist the enemy. Unfortunately, when it comes to our immediate circles of friends, we become complacent in every aspect, including conversation, actions, mindset, and in progression.

I have seen this first hand to its fullest. As a current educator, I've noticed that the well-revered happy hour is one of the staples of being an educator! Often called *choir practice* in emails, the educator happy hour is almost like a badge of honor that you wear. As a new teacher, the first time you are invited to one you feel like, "I've done it! I'm in with the crowd! I'm accepted into the group, and I deserve it! That first week of school was tough." The sad fact is that just past that initial feeling of pride, things rapidly go downhill from there. I've been to several happy hours in years past and regrettably participated in the conversations within those settings. Conversations that usually revolved around complaining about students, complaining about the administration, gossiping about other educators, what's new on Netflix, Hulu, HBO, or whatever the latest streaming thing is, and everything else but the future. I can understand why most people don't talk about the future in regards to big dreams and goals that they have. Most people keep their *future* talk in the realm of what they are doing with their family and work—and that's about it. Why? Because most people's jobs do not give them the flexibility in time or the income to *play at a higher level*.

By *play*, I mean starting that charity in an area you know for sure needs some time, attention, and money, or simply giving to an already existing cause that you believe in. *Play* could be defined as being able to spend more quality time with your family as a whole or individually, so that you, and not this fallen world, can be the main influence in their lives. *Play* can be anything you do with your free time—time away from your job—like having a greater impact in your community than you currently do. That's what I mean by *play at a higher level*.

Boos and Jeers

"I do have an impact in what I do! How dare you say that what I am doing has no impact!" The enemy is a very well-versed chess player. When we hear statements from people like this one, we usually almost instinctively rely on our emotional reactions to guide our next move. This is Satan's preferred way to operate. He wants you to be quick to anger, rage, and offense. Why? Because you will forget to ask questions and you won't take conversations home and think about what was said. Did anyone notice that I mentioned *having a greater impact*? *Greater*. Not having an impact, but having a *greater impact*. I believe that in everything we do, we are impacting one another, whether good or bad. But, at what point is our impact limited because we stop striving for goals and dreams that are *big*? At what point is our impact limited because we become comfortable in our careers and responsibilities? It's not supposed to be "get *me* setup, so I can take care of my family," and that's it. Getting yourself setup is necessary so you can help others as well.

J.K. Rowling didn't write the Harry Potter books because she just wanted to have lots of money so she could move to a secluded mansion and do nothing. She wanted the money so she wouldn't have to focus on the kind of debt that we spend mental energy on daily. She wanted to focus more mental energy on things that matter in the world and use that money to help. Are you surprised to know that she lost her billionaire status at one point because she gave so much of her money away? But again, this is how the Devil works—by opening up a close-friends circle for us, a new job environment, or a new creative outlet to focus on, and then guide us into a place of mediocrity where the goals, dreams, and future desires for ourselves that we once had can slowly be suffocated and die.

This is why it's so important to guard your associative circles—social and business—and keep a mental ledger of how much time and money is being spent and where. You can be led astray even if you believe you are doing good to impact society. There's a great saying by Jim Rohn, who is considered by most to be one of the great entrepreneurs, authors, and motivational speakers of the 20th century. The saying goes, "You are the average of the five people you spend the most time with." Now, due to the interwebs, you can find a whole slew of articles out there refuting this quote. Full transparency, I have not read a single one because I don't care to try to understand why people would think this way. I see that quote for what it is, a clear and blatant warning. Side note, you can also find on the internet why Martin Luther King was a bad person, Mother Teresa wasn't good, and why drinking ice water is bad for you. This internet thing? Real reliable.

Music
Cheers
Let's ... Ask ... A Question!

I figure, at this point, I've asked you so many questions throughout this book that I might as well turn it into a game show.

Have you ever been watching a program where the subject matter requires experts of a swath of different fields to come in and talk about different points to add validity and credence? Maybe it's a zoologist talking about something animal related. Or perhaps it's a doctor talking about a certain type of surgical procedure. Here's the question: *do you think those people interviewed are just your run-of-the-mill technicians in their field, or do you think that the program directors/filmmakers tried their very best to get a top-tier individual*? How do people get to that sort of *next level*? How do people wind up in the annals of history on par with such people as Albert Einstein, Stephen Hawking, Steve Jobs, Jim Rohn, or many others? I would be willing to bet that a lot of it has to do with who they are spending their time with and what relationships they are choosing to cultivate. They are probably chasing those relationships that will help them become better in their career field. Relationships with other highly skilled professionals and thinkers within a given area of study. Why would anyone want to chase, or be around such an association? Because they understand that at some point they will need to continue to sharpen themselves. Not only that, they understand that they can learn from each other. They are open to the possibility that everything they know, may not be all there is to know.

Some of you are reading this and thinking, "I just don't know if I can look at my circle of friends, family, and coworkers that way." To those of you that think like this, I say, good luck! To those of you who are still with me and are realizing that you've never looked at your particular situation this way, a word of warning to you. When my wife and I started learning this idea, we went full auto on that mentality in the wrong direction. We separated ourselves so much from others that we almost crossed into detrimental territory. I am in no way saying that you shouldn't hang out with a multitude of different individuals. Those types of opportunities are always laced with learning potential to understand more about fellow men and women. However, we need to be aware of how much time we spend in those environments, especially if those environments are filled with *floaters*—individuals who don't know what they want out of life, don't think about it, *live in the moment*, who may be inherently selfish, or who would rather complain instead of seeking change. In the simplest of terms, they are floating through life, aimlessly wandering, afraid to take steps out of their comfort zones, or are too skeptical to believe that there are people in this world who would want to help them achieve more.

How does this connect to the idea that we, as a society, have created the perception that Satan is larger than he is or deserves credit for? I took a break from writing this book, at which time, I went out to cut the grass. As I mowed, I thought about this exact question. I began thinking about Satan being in every aspect of our lives, which became the central idea for this book, and thought, "Am I reaching to create the point I have for this particular topic?" I don't think so. I began thinking about that word: *reaching*. Usually when people say, "I think you're reaching," it's usually meant as a way of saying that what you are implying is implausible or is a little too far-fetched to be true. However, after reflecting on the word itself, I think that this definition is incorrect. One of the definitions for *reach* is to pick up and draw toward oneself. Isn't that what we are doing when we think outside of the box, or think higher concepts and thoughts? Drawing toward us a higher level of understanding? With that in mind, I am reaching to think outside of the box for this next point, in hopes that it will elevate thinking and create a discussion.

When we do not actively guard our association and spend time frivolously without being aware of the company, we add to Satan's reputation from a subconscious standpoint. We forget about the threat. We lose focus of the goals I mentioned earlier. We neglect to listen for God's guidance on where our path should lead and the things we are to accomplish. We become complacent, and in doing so, we dismiss the enemy as little more than a villain from a child's comic book. If you ask me, that's a dangerous place to be. The Bible says, "Be alert and of sober mind. Your enemy, the devil prowls around like a roaring lion looking for someone to devour," (1 Pt 5:8-9 NIV). The first line describes the mentality we should have upon waking everyday. Be alert! Many people, and especially Christians, myself included, are not always on alert to the lion that roams, looking for someone to devour.

Of course, we can prevent this subconscious routine by talking openly about it. If we are to combat the enemy and his sneaky ways, then we must be able to confront the topic head on. Even if the thought processes or ideas may seem a little out of the box, they should not be so easily dismissed before we fully explore the potential implications of the idea or thought. Like I said at the start of this chapter and subsequently the middle of it, I was even unsure about talking about this point due to what it is presenting. I know for some people taking stock of their social circles and influences will be hard to swallow. I'll be honest, it's not something that's easy to do. I also believe it's necessary if you want to move forward and start living your life's purpose. Only when we stay alert and council with God, can we begin to have a fulfilled life. It seems purpose and happiness affect a good portion of people today. Many younger generations are growing up and coming to the question, "Is this it?" in regards to working and purpose. Sometimes that question comes early, and to those of you that have asked that early in life, say before 25, kudos to you. You have time to make positive changes in your associations. Sometimes that question comes later in life. Often, it comes too late, when potentially nothing can be done about changing group associations—although, that's only a mindset. With God on your side anything is possible at any age, you only need to believe in Him. "I can do all things through Christ who strengthens me [regardless of age]," (Phil 4:13 NKJV).

8

L'eggo My Ego!

I CAME UP WITH a quote the other day after ruminating on a thought for a while—yes, I am about to quote myself. When you find strength in God, you find that it comes with the ability to speak from personal experience in ways that are complementary without sounding big-headed, haughty, or perhaps . . . with ego . . . (smirk).

The quote goes as follows, *Your greatest battle won't be the hardships of this world, it will be your ego.* As I mentioned earlier in this book, I feel that *ego* stands for *Evil Going On*. As a species, humans have reached the utmost pinnacle of achievements. Achievements that we should honestly be proud of! Why? Because God could have just made duds. He literally could have limited us in every way, especially in the intellect department. I mean look at some of the things we have achieved as a species: space travel (our best one, in my opinion), cures for diseases (also important), physics (talked about this earlier, too), various traveling machines, wireless communication, vinyl records (it always blows my mind!), plumbing and electricity, the list goes on and on. Each of these things is so amazing and such a testament to our God-given minds that it should be further proof of our creator's existence. Unfortunately for some, it's not. Furthermore, if we continue to look and reflect, we can see how the enemy is the subtle reason behind this occurrence. With each achievement, our ego enlarges in size. So much so, that we have gotten to the point where we believe we are the ones in control of our lives, and we alone accomplish much with no help. In a way and to a degree, we are in control of the decisions we make based on the choices presented to us.

I can hear certain people out there saying, "Well, if God's in control, then that means we are not fully in control, which contradicts what the Bible says about our own free will!" However, we do have free will. God is the watchful eye in the sky that helps us by imparting upon us revelations, understanding, epiphanies, and opportunities. Does He ultimately know how our life is going to play out, what paths we will take, and the decisions we will make? Yes! That doesn't mean that He's controlling how our lives play out, telling us what path to take, or forcing us to make decisions. If that were the case, then my life would never have gone the way that it did. It would have never reached a point where I was so broken, so destitute, and so soulfully sad, that I wanted to turn things around and be better. And when I made that choice, when *I made that choice*, what did God do for me? He placed the woman who would become my wife back into my life. She was someone who, like me, had fallen away from God, but who had lived life for a bit and was ready to move forward and do more. She was someone who had mentally matured years earlier than myself. She and I both desired to have the Lord in our lives again. We both needed to make decisions regarding God.

How was I able to make this decision? What was it that changed within me that caused me to see myself for who and what I had become (which was not a good person at all)? I believe it was God calling to me and encouraging me to, "let go your ego." When I let my ego go and said to God, "You take over. You lead my life." I placed God in control. From that point on, I let him guide me, because I no longer cared to guess my way through this life. Instead, I surrendered my own understanding to the One who understands all. Why do you think I mentioned at the beginning of this book that I wanted God's guidance and wisdom in writing this book, and not that of my own? Sadly, the world has strayed greatly from the desire to allow God to lead them through life. As hard as it may be to believe, this includes Christians.

Let me address the intersection of Christians and ego first, because I feel that Christians seem baffled and astonished when it comes to the levels of persecution we receive these days. What I believe we fail to understand here is how our egos play into how we are perceived—our actions and our words. If we are supposed to imitate the life that Christ led to the best of our ability, because let's not forget Christ was perfect, then let us examine this verse of scripture: "As Jesus started on his way, a man ran up to him and fell to his knees before him. 'Good teacher,' he asked, 'what must I do to inherit eternal life?' 'Why do you call me good?' Jesus answered. 'No one is good-except God alone,'" (Mk 10:17-19 NIV).

What an answer! It's amazing to me at times how cool of a cat Jesus is in situations. What's even more interesting here is that Jesus is the embodiment of God. He is God in human form, who came to Earth so He could understand what we go through and be able to empathize with us, while also fulfilling His plan to create an easy way for us to be with Him when we die. And yet, still Jesus defers all glory to God by questioning this man as to why he calls him "good," then following it up with the point that only God alone is good. This is a piece of scripture that, as Christians, we should be keeping with us daily. Now, am I saying that when you are recognized for great achievements in your area of expertise, life, marriage, business, or innovation, that we can't accept the credit that is given? Not at all! God delights when we achieve, when we strive and reach for more. However, we need never forget where to give the first credit, that is to our heavenly Father.

From my perspective, the 21st century Christian is too concerned with ensuring that people know exactly where they stand in regard to Christianity, and if you don't like it, then they will try to change your mind. I think this is wholly the wrong approach. Again, if we look at Jesus' life, no one even really knows who He is until He begins His ministry at about thirty years old. Before that, we only get a few stories that talk about Him when He is a child.

The bulk of Jesus' story begins when His ministry does. Why did so many people come to know the things Jesus believed and spoke with His words? Because He first actively showed love. Love is an action word; to lead with love means that you lead with actions and not just words. Jesus could have said all day long that He loved people and wanted them to know the glory of God, but if His actions didn't line up with the profession that God loves unconditionally, it would have been extremely contradictory.

This does not mean that we should avoid or feel as though we cannot create conversations on controversial concerns and issues within our society. It is within those private personal conversations that we must be careful to keep our egos in check so as not to appear as if we are better than any other person. After all, it is the conversation for which you are appreciative and the openness of perspectives being shared from both sides. We don't have to agree on everything, and yet we can still get along. We shouldn't be roaming around looking for people to argue with over beliefs or morality. Rather, we should lead our lives differently, and, through example, be the difference that will make people ask questions as to why we operate the way that we do. At that point, we can give our own personal testimonies.

Today though, I see too many Christians hubristically leading arguments rather than making inquiries and making references to personal perspective. Why? Because out of all the things in the Bible, ego may be the hardest to control. Those of you that personally know me, know that I am not perfect at the very subject I am discussing. That's because, as much as I would like to be He who is blameless, I am not! All I can do is ask my Heavenly Father for help in this area, daily reflecting on my actions, and engaging in conversations with individuals who have carte blanche to speak into my life and tell me things that are hard to hear. I often wonder, how many of today's Christians are purposefully striving to do these things everyday?

Again, I will interject here to clarify. I'm not perfect in this character trait. I was not good at this for a long, long, long, long,

long time. I am still working on this every single day. I still fail at times to be of this frame of mind. I. Am. Not. Perfect.

There, now that that's cleared up, as Christians, we must get comfortable with the idea of having conversations with one another based on some of the principles I have addressed in this book. I encourage you to have conversations about your word life, associations, ego, definement by God the Father, and our titles of men. What's the likelihood that these conversations and attempts at new understanding will be easy? I'm gonna go out on another limb and say it's pretty close to, if not zero. When I look at Jesus' path though, I see a similar connection. Not in the aspect of ego, association, or any of the other things I just mentioned (Jesus had those on lock), but in the aspect of who He was, what He was about to go through, and how that would take place. Namely that His path to, and on the cross, was not an easy one.

In our efforts to become better Christians, our paths may be strenuous, but they generally don't end in death because of our beliefs. Jesus chose to become the gate by which humankind could be saved. This literally required Him to not only take on every sin that ever existed, but also to die. It could be easy to think, "Well, He's Jesus. He knew from the start what was going on and why. I'll bet He was okay because He knew the outcome. In the end, He would ascend to Heaven and not have to live out his days in this world." Well, let's take a look at scripture. "Going a little farther, he fell with his face to the ground and prayed. 'My father, may this cup be taken from me. Yet not as I will, but as you will,'" (Mt 26:39 NIV). Now I don't know about you, but that doesn't strike me as someone who is okay with the thought that He has to die to fulfill God's plan. What always strikes me about this scripture is Jesus' demeanor. He's not whining or repeatedly asking if maybe there's another way around this whole situation. Nope. He politely prays to God that if it's possible, may the cup be taken from Him, then stating that it's *God's will* that should be done, not his own.

It's funny, I never noticed until upon writing this section that Jesus never asks if the cup can be taken, He states may this cup be taken. Why? I believe that Jesus understood He was not to question

God and His plan for the world. By questioning His own father it would have made Him contradictory to His previous statements to lean not on our own understanding, but rather to lean on God's. Still though, why did He state it then? Because Jesus was still in the flesh. He struggled with the desires of the flesh just like we do. He knew the pain and suffering he was to go through, but wanted God's will to take precedence. He was more disciplined, diligent, and steadfast in His desire to adhere to God's will and not his own. We can see this in Matthew 4:1–11 NIV:

> Then Jesus was led by the Spirit into the wilderness to be tempted by the devil.
>
> After fasting forty days and forty nights, he was hungry. The tempter came to him and said, "If you are the Son of God, tell these stones to become bread." Jesus answered, "It is written: 'Man shall not live on bread alone, but on every word that comes from the mouth of God.'" Then the devil took him to the holy city and had him stand on the highest point of the temple. "If you are the Son of God," he said, "throw yourself down. For it is written: '"He will command his angels concerning you, and they will lift you up in their hands, so that you will not strike your foot against a stone.'" Jesus answered him, "It is also written: 'Do not put the Lord your God to the test.'" Again, the devil took him to a very high mountain and showed him all the kingdoms of the world and their splendor. "All this I will give you," he said, "if you will bow down and worship me." Jesus said to him, "Away from me, Satan! For it is written: 'Worship the Lord your God, and serve him only.'" Then the devil left him, and angels came and attended him.

Then "angels came and attended him." Seems to me like Jesus just got spiritually, emotionally, and physically wrecked through this altercation. Why? He was just as human as you and I because He was in the flesh. My point being that Jesus was human and was tempted just as we are, the only difference being that He persevered throughout, and we should, within the best of our flawed humanistic capabilities, diligently strive to do the same. Being of flesh is something that we have to deal with everyday. We are going to have good days and bad. The important thing is that God's grace abounds, and when we fail to be our best selves or we give into fleshly desires, we can be assured that if we have accepted Jesus into our hearts by a profession of mouth and faith, then God will forgive us. However this also means that we cannot use being of flesh as an excuse over and over again and be okay with it because *God forgives*. We must learn from those moments of flesh, then reflect, spend time in prayer with our Father, and ask for support. This is where we stray. We think, "I got this. I can do it. I'm strong," and you are strong. But you know what? God is stronger! So, why not ask for his assistance right from the get go? Why not stack the deck in your favor from the very beginning? I'll give you a hint . . . *ego*.

Let's move on. I think I have given my Christian brothers and sisters enough to reflect on and talk about with God. See, I don't want you to take my word for it, I want you to talk with God about the things I am discussing here. Search your heart and listen for what our Father has to say. I hope, throughout this book, that I have done His will and not my own. Put forth His thoughts and not mine. That being said, let's shift now and look at the intersectionality of ego with the world.

I said in chapter one that I started writing this book during a pandemic of all things. It's also during one of the most stressful times in our country. Our country is extremely divided on everything from politics, to race, to religion. We are starting to see a breakdown in societal credibility. People who have spent their lives dedicated to the research, understanding, and explanation of a certain topic are labeled either credible or not, solely based on their political or religious views, or even if they don't agree with a current social movement. If you ask me, "What do you think is attributed to the way things are today?" I would have to say, *ego*. It's all about the self today. It's about your perspective and no one else's. Make no mistake, when you bought this book, you were seeking a perspective that was not your own. That's what reading is. A journey into a perspective that's not your own. Now, you don't have to agree with it, but be assured you were seeking more information or insight on the subject. The answer to the aforementioned question above is simple: Ego. It's almost as if our world, and specifically our country, has become filled with such self-conceit that there is no longer such a thing as expertise. No longer do we celebrate each other, or ask questions when we do or create something in a slightly different way. Nope. It seems as though that would be too hard. Don't think this happens on the regular? Pay attention next time you're in conversation with others and someone brings up how they do something that requires skill, knowledge, understanding, or all of the above. How many times have you heard someone explain how they make a traditional cultural meal, and they aren't of that culture or ethnicity? *Boom*! Someone interjects. "That's not how you're supposed to make it. Why would you add this or that? You're ruining a staple of that country or people."

"What's happening?" you think to yourself. You're getting a front row seat to pure, unfiltered, unadulterated *ego*. Is that not what that situation screams? "How dare you call that traditional cuisine. You have no idea what you're talking about. I *am* from that culture, and you are disgracing *our*, nay, *my* heritage!" Now let's look at that conversation through another lens, an *egoless* lens. Person explains a cultural cuisine they make that does not use 100% all the same ingredients. Another person hears this.

"What was your reason for leaving out *x, y, z*?"

"Oh, my stomach does not react well with those particular ingredients. Plus, my children have certain food allergies with those things as well."

"Interesting. What does it do to the overall flavor of the dish itself?"

"Well, funnily enough, back before I knew those ingredients didn't sit well with my stomach, I had actually had the meal a few times. When I finally figured out it was those particular *x,y,z*, ingredients, then I actually took the time to see what I could substitute that wouldn't sacrifice flavor. When I taste it, I don't taste a difference, and even my husband, who is from that area of the world, says he cannot really taste a difference either."

"Really? Wow, that's interesting. Do you ever miss the really really authentic taste of that meal?"

"Sometimes. However, I was talking to a friend of mine, who is a nutritionist, and they said that some of the ingredients that I replaced, actually made the meal that much more healthy. Our family is definitely trying to be more health conscious these days, so that was some welcomed news."

"Wow, really? Would you mind if I got that recipe from you? My husband and I love a lot of the authentic meals from home, but they are not always the best—healthwise—when it comes to some of the main ingredients. I'd love to be able to make them more frequently for my family."

"Of course! What's your email address?"

Can you see the difference when you take an approach that is more inquisitive than accusatory? An approach laced more with a childlike nature than calloused with unadulterated bitterness, reacting with love rather than malice. Even more than those things, what did we just learn about each other? Let's see:

1. A person's stomach does not react well with particular ingredients.
2. Their children have certain food allergies.
3. Person actually had the meal a few times before realizing stomach sensitivity.
4. Did research for new ingredients that wouldn't sacrifice flavor and have a similar taste.
5. Husband is from that particular area and really can't tell the difference in taste with new ingredients.
6. Person has a connection to a nutritionist.
7. New ingredients make cuisine much more healthy and can be served more frequently.
8. Person likes for their family to be health conscious, it's not about disrespect.

9. Other person is also wanting to eat the certain meal/dish more frequently and is happy to hear it's a little more healthy.
10. An exchange of contact information took place.

Look at all the beneficial information and learning that came out of that one exchange simply because we put egos and what we thought we knew about the other persons aside, and who knows, maybe these two people will wind up becoming good friends and share in the trading of recipes for great meals. The possibilities are endless when we approach situations without ego.

Sadly, we as a society are robbing ourselves of such experiences. When we bring ego into the situation, regardless of how much knowledge we have on the subject, we lose a chance to learn about one another and find common ground. This is one of our greatest battles these days. We have begun to frame our society in such a way that constantly reminds us that we don't really know anything. We think our opinions matter more than others', my experience bests your experience. Completely reframing the picture by coming from a place of peaceful inquiry would be much more beneficial in creating a society that is more intimately connected.

What does this mean for those people with expertise? How are we supposed to create a distinction between people who are very credible and proficient, and others who have just dabbled or do not know anything about the topic? Are knowledgeable people supposed to keep their mouths shut and never speak up? Do they state a more comprehensive understanding of certain topics, subjects, and fields, or do they stand in fear of being accused as egotistical? Not at all! When you begin a journey with our Lord and Savior Jesus Christ, a journey of self-improvement, one of discipline in attitude and mind, of character steeped in little or no ego, a few things happen. Aside from knowing that your salvation is secure and you will be living eternally in Heaven one day, you start being able to recognize and appreciate experience coupled with practical application versus pure knowledge alone. "So, people who know a lot are not as good as people with experience?" That's not at all what I am saying. What I am saying is there is a difference in studying to do, and doing what was studied. Let's look at an example. I really like providing examples. I think they are a great way to make subjects tangible and weighted.

My brother is currently a middle school Vice Principal. They call it Assistant Principal these days. I wonder if they deemed *Vice* to be too harsh a term? Or, perhaps it was just time for that title to be updated. Off topic, my apologies. He has been in the field of education for more than 15 years now. Two of those years, he spent on the administration side of education. As for me, I am simply a classroom teacher with no desire to go any higher than a classroom setting. I actually no longer desire to be in the education field altogether, but that is a completely different story. Maybe I will tell that story some day. Point is, I have not familiarized myself with district, state, or federal school policies outside my purview. I do not attend meetings with other heads of education of mine or other districts. I am not a part of the inner circle of the *in the know*. So, when I have a question that may be more general when it comes to thought process or procedure, I ask my brother. Now, every school district does things differently, and he does not sit in on the meetings for my district, but a lot of schools carry similar ideological pedagogies. Also, they must operate by the same state and federal mandated school guidelines. So while he is not specifically within my school district, he can still base an answer to my proposed question with logical reasoning adherent to current state and federal guidelines. I also trust that if he does not have any clue, he will say so. But why do I trust when he does have an answer? Because he goes to meetings throughout the week regarding new and changing procedures. He remains informed of state and federal policies as much as possible. Said more succinctly, he is currently doing the work required of an Assistant Principal. I would consider that an example of applied experience and knowledge within a short time frame. What about the other example I gave, knowledge minus where there may be experience, but it's no longer being applied or sharpened?

Let's look at this example. My dad is an amazing woodworker, as I stated earlier. For the entire time I've known him, he has always been good at fabricating things or creating items. Chairs, tables, paintings, pergolas, decks, electrical wiring, plumbing, the list is rather ridiculous to be honest. However, as he has gotten older he doesn't do some of these things anymore. That doesn't mean that he is not knowledgeable. It just means I could potentially learn another, older, more tested way of doing something that has an updated way for how it's done. I am completely okay with that, because for me, I look at it as though I am adding to my tool box.

When I am working on a household project, I now get to draw upon all the different ways that I have learned, some that are old (from my father) and some new (from Youtube). I utilize all that I've learned and combine this knowledge in such a way that it helps me accomplish my project. In fact, these days, when I call my dad and ask his advice on something, I usually blend it with my idea of what I already know and his knowledge on the topic to see what he thinks. He usually winds up telling me, "Yes you could do it that way. I don't see why that wouldn't work." I think that's because my dad understands he's no longer *in the hunt*, so to speak. When he was younger he would read magazines on carving, woodworking, photography, and would stay up to date with electrical schematics and plumbing plans. That time has passed now, and I believe he knows that. So, when he gives advice, it comes from a place of humbleness. A place that says, "I think they may do this differently these days, but here's what I know."

Most likely, a good percentage of us will never be a part of, or in the rooms where decisions about our country are made, companies are bought and sold, treasonous documents and emails are discussed, or religious heads convene. All we can do is read as much as we can about those topics and, most importantly, engage in conversations that allow us to put all our cards on the table. Conversations that give us different perspectives and views, the sharing of information free from ego and big headedness. Asking questions and never putting ourselves in a place that would personally cause us to be sedentary. By that, I mean a person who never asks pertinent questions, but would rather accept what is being fed to him through the media or other outlets. It may mean

L'EGGO MY EGO!

that you'll have to watch a little less Netflix. It could mean you have to breach your fear of discussing controversial subjects such as politics or religion with your friends and families. God is so much bigger than fear. "For God hath not given us the spirit of fear; but of power, and love, and of a sound mind," (2 Tim 1:7 KJV). It could mean that you have to swallow your pride and admit at times that you're wrong. You voted wrong. You thought wrong. You said something wrong. You supported the wrong cause. An admission that comes from a true heart, and not because you were pressured by another's hatred, disdain, or lack of a self-image, is worth its weight in gold. These days, for me, when someone can come back and say, "Hey, I was wrong, or I was blind to this, but I get it now. I'm sorry." That is the highest honor one can receive. It shows me the characteristic of humility that I know we all possess. God is the only one who can help us with humility in the way that we need. My wife can do little to help me in this area of life. However, sometimes that little bit still exacerbates the situation. Our friends can only do so much, as can our families. Only God can instill in us the peace that we need to conquer ego.

I have ended every chapter in this book with ways in which the topic of each chapter connects to the larger idea that we are making the Devil too big in our society in how we approach certain aspects of being and living. Therefore, I would like to end this chapter differently and with a question. What part do you think ego plays in increasing the persona of the Devil and creating the picture that he is larger and more menacing than he actually is?

9

A Final Word

My sincerest hope is that you have found the perspectives in this book to be starting points for greater contemplation and conversations. Ultimately, that is my goal. As someone who was born again early in life, who left to embrace the world only to return broken, beat up, and feeling of no value, I know how much my Lord Jesus Christ has helped me to become a better person, not only in flesh but in spirit as well. With Him, I have developed into a man my wife is proud to call husband and running mate for the race of life. I'm not just tooting my own horn here, she has personally told me this. I have become a better son, able to embrace a once rocky relationship with my own father. Where there was once impatience and anger, there is now a loving relationship and a strength found in acknowledging the differences in our perspectives. Even with all that said, Christ has done even more by helping me with my personal issues of anger and pornography. He has done His work to mold and shape me into the man of character He desires me to become. It's a process that will never be finished until I meet my Savior face to face. With His help, I will make progress everyday. As he teaches me, I grow but remain humbled by His tutelage.

One of the things that makes our relationship with Christ so special is that He is a teacher that is always there and always good.

A Final Word

For some, looking at this life as a process of constantly learning and changing can be a daunting realization. This is partly why I believe people settle so easily into routine. One doesn't have to change a routine. It's constant. It's the same, and it's been learned, and I'm comfortable. *Warning*: This doesn't mean all routines are bad!

The thought of constantly growing and changing was, and is still difficult for me. It is a mindset that God has had to develop within me over time, and is still cultivating to this day. There are definitely times where I don't want to read, grow my perspective, listen to my wife, speak positively over my life, be salt, or be light to this world. Those are the times that my relationship with my Heavenly Father is most important. I rely on Him to rid me of thoughts and feelings that come from the enemy and to give me strength and direction for the day. What's even more beautiful about the relationship is that if for some reason I am not my best that day, maybe I'm more harsh than I need to be toward my wife or some undeserving stranger, I can go back to my *teacher* and those who I've wronged and ask for forgiveness. He gives me grace and understands the complexities, temptations, and stressors of this world. God knows and understands what we go through in this life. He knows we won't always make the right choices. Making wrong decisions can lead to sin. Why do you think He sent His son Jesus Christ? It was the only way in which He could offer salvation to mankind.

This does not mean that I purposefully walk through life actively trying to be dishonest in my dealings, and it's not a *get out of jail free* card. It becomes a *get out of jail free* card when people do not reflect, come to understand, learn, and change what they are asking God's forgiveness for. I think this is why the world views Christians the way that they do regarding forgiveness and our relationship with God. Too many people are using the, "Well, God forgives, so I'm good." Yes, He does forgive. However, I believe He is also expecting that you learn at the same time and change your ways.

Let's look at an example of this in practicum. I mentioned earlier that God has helped me with many things. My top two biggest areas of refinement, hands down, have been that of anger and pornography. I would like to discuss the latter. "Oh my gosh, he said *pornography!*" Yes, I did. It's something that exists, and if we can't talk about it, then we choose by default to let it grow out of control with our sons and daughters. If I tell my wife that I am praying to God for his help but I keep returning to pornography, over a period of time, I begin to take all meaning and importance away from the act of praying and seeking God's help. What do I mean? It becomes worthless. It could even potentially create a rift in my wife's mind and cause doubt that prayer and God Himself actually work. (I know my wife, and this would never happen, but you do hear stories like this of people doubting their faith due to situations like this.) Of course, this doesn't mean that through my struggle I am going to be perfect. I should stay in communication with my wife and talk about when I feel the enemy coming against me with thoughts and urges, and we can pray for God's help together. With God's help, at some point, I should be able to shake pornography altogether.

My point with all of this is to say that I understand life is inherently difficult. It's inherent because we inherited that from Adam and Eve. However, God's gift to us is free will—the ability to make choices—no matter the circumstances. Historically, there have been many accounts of people who had extremely tough lives, and yet, they managed to prosper. How'd they do it? My hope is that they leaned on God and put their faith in Him. Still, if they didn't, they utilized the gift of choice. They chose to view their hardships through a lens of positivity. I like to call it, being *logically positive*. This means that when bad things happen, I do not ignore that the bad thing has happened. I am aware and understand what has just transpired, but do not allow it to forever guide the trajectory of my life. Things *will* get better. Things *will* turn around. Things *will* change and become good again. The hardship is limited to the amount of time we allow it to be a hardship. You can curse the world and God for being born blind or without legs, or

A Final Word

you can rise above and inspire others by showing them that even without legs, you can still skateboard. Even without sight, you can still paint a beautiful painting or achieve something that is heavily dependent on sight.

If you have felt like these days there is nowhere else to turn, as if the world has become too complicated and uncertain, then I invite you to pray a prayer of salvation with me right now. It doesn't matter where you are or what time of day it is. If you are feeling as though you may be a *floater*, that your life is missing something, maybe you have all the money in the world, or the exact opposite, and still you find yourself empty, then I invite you to say the following words out loud and with a sincerity of heart. The Bible says that we must confess Jesus as Lord and Savior with our mouths and hearts. "For it is with your heart that you believe and are justified, and it is with your mouth that you profess your faith and are saved," (Rom 10:10 NIV). It is not enough for us to just think in our heads that Jesus is Lord, but we must openly confess this to be true. So, if you feel so compelled, say these words with me now out loud:

> *Dear Heavenly Father,*
> *I confess right now, without any shame, embarrassment, or uncertainty that your son, Jesus Christ, came to this world and died for my sins. I believe and understand that upon His dying, all my sins were washed away and my debt was paid. Your word says that by my confession, I am saved by the blood of Christ and will spend my eternity with you in Heaven. I believe, as I confess Jesus now, that His Spirit is coming into my heart. Lord, I know that with your help, I will begin to see miraculous changes in my life. I praise your name and give myself completely to you, so that you may live through me as an example of a changed life. Thank you for all you have done, all you will do, and your never-ending grace and forgiveness. I pray all this in your mighty and exalted name,*
> *Amen.*

If you just prayed those words out loud, I want to be the first to congratulate you! You have taken the first step in having a more complete and fulfilled life through Christ Jesus. I want to encourage you now to do two things:

1. Go tell a friend. When we make professions of faith, it's not something we should ever be afraid to admit. It's like getting that promotion at work or finally finishing that degree, it's something to be celebrated! So, go find someone that you know who, even if they haven't made a profession of faith, they won't try to downplay it or be negative toward it. Rather, they will celebrate with you!

2. Go get yourself a Bible and seek out a fellowship of individuals who can help guide you as a newly professed Christian and follower of Christ. Begin getting into God's word so that you can cultivate that relationship with Him, and He can begin to instill in you wisdom, understanding, and revelation. Later, you may also look into getting baptized—even though baptism is not a necessary step for salvation. Some people, like my wife, choose to be baptized as an extra step in their faith journey, and some choose not to be baptized. It's entirely preferential. The important piece was the profession of faith you made earlier.

I sincerely hope that this book encourages you to take stock of your life, analyze, and reflect on things. That it encourages you to have conversations with others about these topics, mindsets, and situations. Above all, I hope that you were able to come to know God as I know Him and am still learning of Him, all His goodness and grace.

The enemy would like you to think we are alone in this world. God helps us know that we are not!

May God bless you all.

www.ingramcontent.com/pod-product-compliance
Lightning Source LLC
Chambersburg PA
CBHW071158090426
42736CB00012B/2371